WeightWatchers®

Pizza, Pizza

150 deliciously dazzling ways
to make everyone's favorite pie

**WEIGHT WATCHERS
PUBLISHING GROUP**

Creative and Editorial Director
Nancy Gagliardi
Art Director
Ed Melnitsky
Production Manager
Alan Biederman
Office Manager/Publishing Assistant
Jenny Laboy-Brace

Food Editor
Eileen Runyan, M.S.
Recipe Developers
Cynthia DePersio
Maureen Luchejko
Sarah Reynolds
Eileen Runyan, M.S.

Photographer
James Baigrie
Food Stylist
Michael Pederson
Prop Stylist
Lynda White

Designer
Mim Adkins

On the cover:
Zucchini-Pomodoro Pizza,
page 169

A Word About Weight Watchers

Since 1963, Weight Watchers has grown from a handful of people to millions of enrollments annually. Today, Weight Watchers is recognized as the leading name in safe and sensible weight control. Weight Watchers members form a diverse group, from youths to senior citizens, attending meetings virtually around the globe. Weight-loss and weight-management results vary by individual, but we recommend that you attend Weight Watchers meetings, follow the Weight Watchers food plan, and participate in regular physical activity. For a Weight Watchers meeting near you, call 800-651-6000. Also, check out *Weight Watchers* Magazine (for subscription information call 800-978-2400) and visit us at our Web site: WeightWatchers.com.

Icons

- hot/fiery
- no cooking
- one pot
- 20 minutes or less
- vegetarian

Additional photography: Mitch Hrdlicka/PhotoDisc; Benjamin F. Fink Jr./PhotoDisc; Jean-Blaise Hall/Pictor; EyeWire Collection; Burke/Triolo Productions; Nick Koudis/PhotoDisc; and Doug Menuez/PhotoDisc

Introduction

Pizza: It's simple (bread and cheese), portable (fold and eat), and a complete meal (protein, carb, and veggie). What's not to love? And love our pizzas, we Americans do. In survey after survey, it's a top-rated snack/craving food, leading a list that includes our other beloved obsessions, chocolate and chips. But what we know as pizza is a far cry from the razor-thin crusts topped with slices of fresh tomato that made their way from Naples.

Today, pizza is a concept. Toppings can be as diverse as potatoes to pineapple. And while pizza purists may cringe, the creative rejoice. There's just one problem: size. A typical slice of a pie, complete with thick sauce, gooey cheese, and all the extras, tops the fat and calories charts. In fact, *Pizza, Pizza 150 Deliciously Dazzling Ways with Everyone's Favorite Pie* was inspired by our quest to have a slice that wouldn't bankrupt the *POINTS* account. Thus, here are more than 150 wonderfully delicious recipes that take pizza to new heights. We kept a watchful eye on portion size—the majority of these are a mere *5 POINTS* a slice.

There truly is something for everyone in *Pizza, Pizza 150 Deliciously Dazzling Ways with Everyone's Favorite Pie:* pizzas for traditionalists, including a foolproof recipe for the dough-phobic (Basic Doughs and Sauces). We've got pizzas for fire-lovers (Pizzas Off the Grill), pizza for the time-challenged (Pizza Pronto), pizzas for people who love the protein (Hearty Pizzas)—and don't (Veggie Slices). Don't laugh but we even have pizzas to satisfy a sweet tooth (Sweet Slices). What's more, we've included a slew of light salads and sides (Pizza Sidekicks), giving recommendations for which pizzas to pair with them.

Everything is fair game. We have pizzas made from tortillas, English muffins, even French bread. Toppings range from the traditional (a grating of fresh cheese) to the unorthodox (pizza with sole, anyone?). Naturally, we've also included pizza-making how-tos, easy tips, and complete nutrition information, so your pizzas not only look and taste good, but they're also good for you.

Enjoy!

Nancy Gagliardi
Creative and Editorial Director

Contents

1 • Basic Doughs and Sauces 6

2 • Appetizer Pizzas
Great Starters or Light Meals 14

3 • Hearty Pizzas
Pies for Big Appetites 34

4 • Coastal Combos
Shrimp, Scallops, and More Favorite Toppings 56

5 • Veggie Slices
No-Meat Pizzas 76

6 • Pizza Deluxe
Mega-Delicious Toppings 96

7 • Pizzas Off the Grill
Crisp Pies with a Smoky Touch 118

8 • Pizza Pronto
10 Minutes or Less—No Kidding! 140

9 • Special Delivery
Mix-and-Match Make-Ahead Toppings 160

10 • Pizza Sidekicks
Salads and Sides to Pair with Your Pie 180

11 • Sweet Slices
"Pizzas" for Dessert 200

Basic Doughs and Sauces

Pizza Perfect

You want to give your family a delicious homemade pizza. We want to give you the know-how to do that. Let these few tricks of the trade be your guide:

The Deal on Dough:
- We use all-purpose flour to make our pizza dough, but if extra-chewy is what you're looking for, use bread flour, which is high in gluten. If extra-crispy is your favorite, use our Semolina Pizza Dough (page 11).
- Flours absorb liquid differently, so start with the smaller amount called for in the recipe when making the dough. If the dough is a little sticky, knead extra flour into it until it becomes smooth and springy.
- You'll find the dough much easier to work with if you let it come to room temperature before rolling it out or stretching it to the desired shape. This is particularly true of store-bought dough, which generally doesn't roll out or stretch as easily as the homemade version.
- If, after rolling out the dough, it shrinks back in size, let it rest for 1 minute. Then continue to roll to the desired size, transfer to the pizza pan, and gently pull the dough back into shape.

Tips for Topping
- To avoid a soggy crust, don't be tempted to overload the pizza with toppings, and once you've spread the topping on the dough, bake the pizza right away.
- For pizza with a golden, puffed rim, spread the topping to about ½ inch from the edge of the dough. This allows the uncovered edges of the dough to rise and brown as it bakes.

Baking the Pizza
- We bake many of our pizzas on the bottom rack of a hot oven, so the crust browns nicely and cooks through.
- Thicker or stuffed pizzas take longer to cook through and are cooked in the middle of a moderately hot oven, for a longer time.
- Toward the end of the cooking time, peek inside the oven and rotate the pizza if it is baking unevenly. Lift the crust, too. If the bottom is still pale but the topping is almost done, reduce the temperature and bake the pizza longer.
- For piping-hot pizza, serve only part of it and leave the remainder in the turned-off oven.

Basic Pizza Dough

Makes 2 (12-inch) pizza crusts (6 servings each)

This dough makes enough for two pizzas, so you can freeze half the dough for another day. If you freeze it, thaw it in the refrigerator overnight, or on the counter for 1½ hours. Unlike other bread dough, pizza dough needs to rise only once. After rising, simply punch it down, then let it rest for 15 minutes before rolling or stretching to the desired shape. If you like, you can let the dough rise in a floured zip-close freezer bag in the refrigerator overnight. You'll find it easiest to roll out or stretch bread dough when it's at room temperature.

1½ cups warm
   (105-115°F) water
1 teaspoon sugar
1 package active
   dry yeast
1 tablespoon olive oil
4¼ cups all-purpose flour
1½ teaspoons salt

1. Combine the water and sugar in a 2-cup measuring jug. Sprinkle in the yeast and let stand until foamy, about 5 minutes. Stir in the oil.

2. Combine the flour and salt in a food processor. With the machine running, scrape the yeast mixture through the feed tube; pulse until the dough forms a ball, about 1 minute. If necessary, turn the dough onto a lightly floured surface and knead briefly until smooth and elastic.

3. Spray a large bowl with nonstick spray; put the dough in the bowl. Cover the bowl lightly with plastic wrap and let the dough rise in a warm spot until it doubles in size, about 1 hour.

4. Punch down the dough, then cut in half. Refrigerate or freeze in floured zip-close freezer bags at this point or use as directed in the recipe.

Per serving (½2 of dough): 174 Cal, 2 g Fat, 0 g Sat Fat, 0 mg Chol, 292 mg Sod, 34 g Carb, 1 g Fib, 5 g Prot, 7 mg Calc. **POINTS: 3.**

 If Mixing by Hand: To make bread by hand, combine the water, sugar, and yeast in a large bowl; set aside until foamy. Stir in the oil, flour, and salt until the dough starts to gather around the spoon. Turn the dough onto a lightly floured surface; knead until the dough is smooth and elastic, about 10 minutes.

Cornmeal Pizza Dough

Pizzas with a Mexican influence are terrific made on a cornmeal crust. Substitute 1 cup cornmeal for 1 cup of the all-purpose flour.

Per serving (1/12 of dough): 178 Cal, 2 g Fat, 0 g Sat Fat, 0 mg Chol, 292 mg Sod, 35 g Carb, 2 g Fib, 5 g Prot, 6 mg Calc. *POINTS: 3.*

Semolina Pizza Dough

Using part semolina flour makes a crispier-crusted pizza. If you can't find semolina flour, use farina cereal. Substitute 1½ cups semolina flour for 1½ cups of the all-purpose flour.

Per serving (1/12 of dough): 192 Cal, 2 g Fat, 0 g Sat Fat, 0 mg Chol, 292 mg Sod, 38 g Carb, 2 g Fib, 6 g Prot, 8 mg Calc. *POINTS: 4.*

Whole-Wheat Pizza Dough

Whole-wheat flour makes a higher-fiber, more nutritious crust. Substitute 1¼ cups whole-wheat flour for 1¼ cups of the all-purpose flour.

Per serving (1/12 of dough): 177 Cal, 2 g Fat, 0 g Sat Fat, 0 mg Chol, 292 mg Sod, 34 g Carb, 3 g Fib, 6 g Prot, 5 mg Calc. *POINTS: 3.*

Basic Tomato Sauce

Makes 6 cups

This is probably the most well-loved and well-used of all sauces—whether you hail from an Italian background or not. Use it for pizzas, pasta dishes, and to sauce meats and fish of all kinds. You can pack the sauce in 2-cup portions to keep on hand in the refrigerator for up to three days or in the freezer for up to three months.

1 tablespoon extra-virgin
olive oil

2 onions, chopped

4 garlic cloves, chopped

3 pounds (about 18) plum
tomatoes, chopped, or 2
(28-ounce) cans Italian
plum tomatoes, drained
and chopped

¼ cup dry red wine

2 tablespoons tomato paste

1 tablespoon chopped fresh
oregano, or 1 teaspoon
dried

1 teaspoon sugar

½ teaspoon salt

¼ teaspoon freshly ground
pepper

⅛ teaspoon crushed red
pepper (optional)

1. Heat a nonstick Dutch oven over medium heat. Swirl in the oil, then add the onions and garlic. Cook, stirring frequently, until golden, about 10 minutes.

2. Add the tomatoes, wine, tomato paste, oregano, sugar, salt, ground pepper, and crushed red pepper (if using); bring to a boil. Reduce the heat and simmer, uncovered, until the flavors are blended and the sauce is slightly thickened, about 25 minutes.

Per serving (½ cup): 48 Cal, 2 g Fat, 0 g Sat Fat, 0 mg Chol, 109 mg Sod, 8 g Carb, 2 g Fib, 1 g Prot, 14 mg Calc. *POINTS: 1.*

Roasted Tomato Sauce

Makes 4½ cups

For a truly intense tomato flavor, roasting is the way to go. Once you try this sauce and see how delicious and easy it is, you'll use it over and over again. It's great in many of the pizza recipes in this book and on pasta, too. Use Vidalia onion for sweetness, otherwise substitute 2 regular onions and sprinkle ½ teaspoon sugar over them before baking. You can pack the sauce in 2-cup portions to keep on hand in the refrigerator for up to three days or in the freezer for up to three months.

3 pounds (about 18) plum tomatoes, cut in fourths lengthwise

1 large Vidalia onion, halved lengthwise, then sliced crosswise

1 tablespoon balsamic vinegar

3 garlic cloves, minced

¾ teaspoon salt

¼ teaspoon freshly ground pepper

1. Adjust the racks to divide the oven in thirds. Preheat the oven to 375°F. Spray 2 large nonstick baking pans with olive-oil nonstick spray.

2. Arrange the tomatoes and onion in single layers on the pans. Sprinkle with the vinegar, garlic, salt, and pepper, then spray lightly with olive-oil nonstick spray. Roast, switching the pans from one shelf to the other halfway through the cooking, until the tomatoes and onion are lightly browned and have an intense, sweet aroma, 50–55 minutes.

3. Transfer the tomatoes and onion to a food processor; pulse until the mixture is combined but still a little chunky.

Per serving (½ cup): 39 Cal, 1 g Fat, 0 g Sat Fat, 0 mg Chol, 208 mg Sod, 9 g Carb, 2 g Fib, 2 g Prot, 13 mg Calc. **POINTS: 0.**

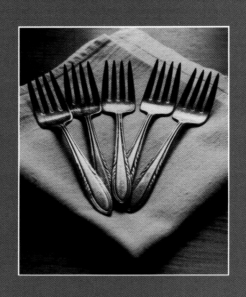

Appetizer Pizzas

Great Starters or Light Meals

Antipasto-Stuffed Focaccia

Makes 12 servings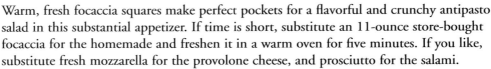

Warm, fresh focaccia squares make perfect pockets for a flavorful and crunchy antipasto salad in this substantial appetizer. If time is short, substitute an 11-ounce store-bought focaccia for the homemade and freshen it in a warm oven for five minutes. If you like, substitute fresh mozzarella for the provolone cheese, and prosciutto for the salami.

2¼ cups all-purpose flour

1 (¼-ounce) package quick-rise yeast

¾ teaspoon salt

¾ cup + 2 tablespoons very warm water (120–130°F)

1 (7-ounce) jar roasted red peppers, rinsed, drained, and cut into strips

24 pitted black and green olives, coarsely chopped

3 tablespoons fat-free Italian dressing

1 garlic clove, minced

1 tablespoon grated Parmesan cheese

1 cup grape tomatoes, halved

1 large celery stalk, sliced

¼ small red onion, thinly sliced

3 ounces sliced provolone cheese, diced

1 ounce thinly sliced salami, diced

1. Combine the flour, yeast, and salt in a food processor. With the machine running, pour the warm water through the feed tube. Pulse until the dough forms a ball, about 1 minute. Turn the dough onto a lightly floured surface and knead briefly until smooth and elastic. Cover lightly with plastic wrap and let rest 10 minutes.

2. Spray a 9 × 13-inch baking pan with olive-oil nonstick spray. Place the dough in the pan and press with fingertips to cover the bottom of the pan. Cover the pan with plastic wrap and let the dough rise in a warm spot until it almost doubles in size, about 45 minutes.

3. Meanwhile, combine the roasted peppers, olives, dressing, and garlic in a large bowl; set aside to marinate.

4. Preheat the oven to 425°F. Spray the dough with nonstick spray. Sprinkle with the Parmesan cheese. Bake until browned, 20–25 minutes. Remove the focaccia from the pan and let cool on a rack.

5. Add the tomatoes, celery, onion, provolone cheese, and salami to the roasted pepper mixture. Cut the focaccia into 12 squares, then split each square in half horizontally. Fill each square with about ⅓ cup of the antipasto mixture.

Per serving (1 square): 144 Cal, 4 g Fat, 2 g Sat Fat, 9 mg Chol, 412 mg Sod, 21 g Carb, 2 g Fib, 6 g Prot, 76 mg Calc. *POINTS: 3.*

 tip Serving fewer than 12 people and you have leftover focaccia? Store it in the freezer, ready to thaw when you need a great sandwich bread.

Flatbread with Smoked Ham and Cheese

Makes 16 servings

Stuffed with a simple, spicy filling, this tasty flatbread—topped with whole parsley leaves and shredded Asiago cheese—is baked crisp, then cut into small rectangles, making it an elegant choice for a cocktail party.

2 ounces sliced smoked ham, finely diced

2 ounces smoked Gouda or cheddar cheese, finely diced

½ teaspoon minced fresh rosemary, or ¼ teaspoon dried

¼ teaspoon crushed red pepper

¼ teaspoon freshly ground pepper

½ recipe (about 1 pound) Basic Pizza Dough (page 10), at room temperature

¼ cup flat-leaf parsley leaves

¼ cup finely shredded Asiago cheese

1. Combine the ham, Gouda cheese, rosemary, crushed red pepper, and ground pepper in a small bowl; set aside. Spray a 10 × 15-inch jelly-roll pan with nonstick spray.

2. Sprinkle a work surface lightly with flour. Turn the dough onto the surface; knead lightly. With a floured rolling pin, roll into a 13 × 18-inch rectangle. Starting at a short side, brush half the rectangle lightly with water.

3. Sprinkle the ham mixture evenly over the brushed half of the dough, up to ½ inch from the edges. Fold the uncovered dough over the filling so the edges meet. Press the edges firmly to seal. Transfer the rectangle to the jelly-roll pan. Gently press the top of the dough all over until it covers the bottom of the pan. Lightly spray the top of the dough with nonstick spray; cover with plastic wrap and let rest 15 minutes.

4. Preheat the oven to 450°F. Prick the top of the dough with a fork all over at 2-inch intervals. Bake until the crust is golden, 12–14 minutes. If the dough puffs up while baking, prick a few times with a fork. Arrange the parsley evenly over the top and sprinkle with the Asiago cheese. Return to the oven until the cheese melts, about 1 minute. Slide the flatbread onto a rack to cool slightly. Transfer to a cutting board and cut into 32 rectangles. Serve warm or at room temperature.

Per serving (2 pieces): 92 Cal, 2 g Fat, 1 g Sat Fat, 6 mg Chol, 227 mg Sod, 13 g Carb, 1 g Fib, 4 g Prot, 53 mg Calc. *POINTS: 2.*

 tip To make rolling and stretching the pizza dough easier, we recommend (in all our recipes) letting the pizza dough come to room temperature. This is especially important in recipes such as this, where the dough is rolled out very thin.

Herbed Flatbreads
with Roast-Garlic
Cheese Spread

Herbed Flatbreads with Roast-Garlic Cheese Spread

Makes 12 servings

Serve these tasty wedges of flatbread with their spread of creamy roasted garlic and sun-dried tomatoes at your next party. The spread can be made up to three days ahead and stored, covered, in the refrigerator.

8 large garlic cloves, peel left on

6 sun-dried tomatoes (not oil-packed)

1 (8-ounce) package nonfat cream cheese, softened

⅓ cup finely chopped fresh basil

⅓ cup grated Parmesan cheese

¼ teaspoon freshly ground pepper

1½ teaspoons minced fresh rosemary, or ½ teaspoon dried

½ recipe (about 1 pound) Basic Pizza Dough (page 10), at room temperature

1. Adjust the racks to divide the oven in thirds. Preheat the oven to 350°F. Wrap the garlic in foil and bake until soft, about 45 minutes. Let cool.

2. Combine the sun-dried tomatoes with enough boiling water to cover in a small bowl. Let stand until softened, about 15 minutes. Drain the tomatoes, then finely chop.

3. Squeeze the garlic pulp into a bowl, then mash with a fork. Add the tomatoes, cream cheese, 2 tablespoons of the basil, 2 tablespoons of the Parmesan cheese, and the pepper. Stir until well blended, spoon into a crock or ramekin, and set aside.

4. Increase the oven temperature to 450°F. Spray 2 baking sheets with nonstick spray. In a small bowl, combine the remaining generous 3 tablespoons basil, the remaining 3 tablespoons Parmesan cheese, and the rosemary; set aside.

5. Sprinkle a work surface lightly with flour. Turn the dough onto the surface; knead lightly. With a lightly floured rolling pin, roll into a 12-inch square. Brush the dough lightly with water, then sprinkle with the basil mixture. Roll up from one side, jelly-roll style, and pinch the seam to seal. Cut the roll into 12 slices. Roll each slice, cut-side down, into a 4-inch circle. Place the circles ½ inch apart on the baking sheets. Bake until golden brown, 10–12 minutes. Cut each circle into 4 wedges, making a total of 48 wedges. Serve warm with the cheese spread.

Per serving (4 wedges and 4 teaspoons cheese spread): 127 Cal, 2 g Fat, 1 g Sat Fat, 2 mg Chol, 359 mg Sod, 21 g Carb, 1 g Fib, 7 g Prot, 71 mg Calc. *POINTS: 3.*

Classic Pizza Pissaladière

Makes 16 servings

Pissaladière—a tart or pizza native to Nice, France—is traditionally a crust topped with golden sautéed onions, then garnished with anchovies and niçoise olives. Our version, embellished with a rich and intense roasted-tomato sauce, makes a satisfying appetizer for a large group.

3 pounds onions, thinly sliced

4 garlic cloves, minced

1 tablespoon balsamic vinegar

2 teaspoons minced fresh thyme

¼ teaspoon salt

¼ teaspoon ground pepper

½ recipe (about 1 pound) Basic Pizza Dough— whole-wheat variation (page 11), at room temperature

1 cup Roasted Tomato Sauce (page 13)

1 tomato, seeded and diced

12 niçoise or other small oil-cured black olives, pitted and halved

6 flat anchovies, rinsed and halved lengthwise

2 tablespoons coarsely chopped fresh basil, or flat-leaf parsley

1. Combine the onions and ¼ cup water in a large non-stick skillet; bring to a boil. Reduce the heat and simmer, covered, until softened, about 15 minutes. Stir in the garlic, vinegar, thyme, salt, and pepper. Increase the heat to medium and cook, uncovered, stirring frequently, until very soft and browned, about 35 minutes. Set aside to cool.

2. Preheat the oven to 500°F. Spray a large baking sheet with nonstick spray.

3. Sprinkle a work surface lightly with flour. Turn the dough onto the surface; knead lightly. With a lightly floured rolling pin, roll into a 12 × 15-inch rectangle. Transfer the dough to the baking sheet, gently pulling the dough back to a 12 × 15-inch rectangle.

4. Spread the Roasted Tomato Sauce over the dough, up to ½ inch from the edges. Spread the onion mixture evenly over the sauce. Arrange the tomato, olives, and anchovies decoratively on top of the onions. Bake until the crust is browned at the edges, 12–15 minutes. Slide the pizza onto a large cutting board, sprinkle with the basil, then cut into 32 rectangles.

Per serving (2 pieces): 107 Cal, 1 g Fat, 0 g Sat Fat, 1 mg Chol, 214 mg Sod, 21 g Carb, 3 g Fib, 4 g Prot, 30 mg Calc. *POINTS: 2.*

Smoked Salmon Pizza Slices with Wasabi Cream and Chives

Makes 12 servings

A version of this pizza was popularized in California by *über*-chef, Wolfgang Puck. If you are short on time, use six 6-inch flour tortillas instead of the pizza dough and bake with the onions for only five minutes. Wasabi, a sharp, pungent Japanese horseradish, comes in paste and powdered form—either variety works in this recipe.

½ recipe (about 1 pound) Basic Pizza dough (page 10), at room temperature

1 small red onion, halved lengthwise, then thinly sliced crosswise

3 tablespoons light sour cream

1½ teaspoons water

¾ teaspoon wasabi powder

4 ounces thinly sliced smoked salmon, cut into strips

1 plum tomato, seeded and diced

2 tablespoons snipped fresh chives

1. Arrange one rack on the bottom rung of the oven. Preheat the oven to 500°F. Spray a large baking sheet with nonstick spray.

2. Sprinkle a work surface lightly with flour. Turn the dough onto the surface; knead lightly. Divide the dough into 6 pieces. With a lightly floured rolling pin, roll each piece into a 5-inch circle. Place the circles on the baking sheet. Divide the onion among the circles; lightly spray the onion with nonstick spray. Bake the circles on the bottom rack of the oven until crisp and lightly browned, 8–10 minutes.

3. Meanwhile, to make the wasabi cream, combine the sour cream, water, and wasabi powder in a small bowl; whisk until blended.

4. Arrange the smoked salmon evenly over the crusts, then sprinkle with the tomato and chives. Drizzle with the wasabi cream. Cut each circle into 6 slices, making a total of 36 slices.

Per serving (3 slices): 107 Cal, 2 g Fat, 0 g Sat Fat, 4 mg Chol, 222 mg Sod, 18 g Carb, 1 g Fib, 4 g Prot, 11 mg Calc. *POINTS: 2.*

 tip   For a fancy, restaurant-style presentation, place the wasabi cream in a small plastic food storage bag; snip one corner and pipe the cream on the pizzas.

Nacho Pizzas with Fresh Chipotle-Tomato Salsa

Makes 12 servings

Pizza dough made with cornmeal or semolina gives crunch to these "nachos." Mexican cheese blends are available in supermarkets and can contain anywhere from two to four cheeses. Look for the light version of whichever cheese blend you prefer, or use a combination of reduced-fat cheddar and Monterey Jack cheeses. *Chipotles en adobo* come in cans and add hot, smoky flavor to foods. Find them in Latin American markets and some large supermarkets.

3 ripe tomatoes, seeded and chopped

3 tablespoons finely chopped red onion

3 tablespoons chopped fresh cilantro

1 tablespoon fresh lime juice

1 chipotle en adobo, seeded and minced

¼ teaspoon salt

½ recipe (about 1 pound) Basic Pizza Dough—cornmeal or semolina variation (page 11), at room temperature

1¼ cups shredded light Mexican 4-cheese blend (cheddar, Monterey Jack, asadero, and queso blanco)

2 teaspoons taco seasoning

1. Adjust the racks to divide the oven in thirds. Preheat the oven to 500°F. Spray 2 baking sheets with nonstick spray.

2. To make the salsa, combine the tomatoes, onion, cilantro, lime juice, chipotle, and salt in a bowl; set aside.

3. Sprinkle a work surface lightly with flour. Turn the dough onto the surface; knead lightly. Divide the dough into 6 pieces. With a lightly floured rolling pin, roll each piece of dough into a 6-inch circle. Transfer the dough circles to the baking sheets.

4. Combine the cheese and taco seasoning in a bowl. Sprinkle the dough circles with the cheese mixture. Bake until the crusts are lightly browned, about 8 minutes. Slide the circles onto a large cutting board, then cut each circle into 6 wedges, making a total of 36 wedges. Serve warm with the salsa.

Per serving (3 wedges and 2 tablespoons salsa): 143 Cal, 4 g Fat, 2 g Sat Fat, 11 mg Chol, 323 mg Sod, 20 g Carb, 1 g Fib, 6 g Prot, 93 mg Calc. *POINTS: 3.*

 tip The salsa is best if the flavors are allowed to develop for at least 20 minutes before serving. It will keep, refrigerated, for up to three days.

Nacho Pizzas with Fresh Chipotle-Tomato Salsa

Spicy Mixed-Pepper Pizza Wedges

Makes 10 servings

Aged Monterey Jack cheese is firmer-textured and sharper-flavored than regular Monterey Jack cheese. It is popular on the West Coast, but can be found in specialty cheese stores throughout the country. Substitute Parmesan or sharp cheddar cheese if it's more readily available.

2 teaspoons olive oil

1 large red bell pepper, seeded and thinly sliced

1 large green bell pepper, seeded and thinly sliced

1 medium red onion, halved lengthwise, then thinly sliced crosswise

2 jalapeño peppers, seeded and thinly sliced (wear gloves to prevent irritation)

¼ teaspoon salt

3 garlic cloves, minced

2 teaspoons hot pepper sauce

1 medium tomato, diced

½ recipe (about 1 pound) Basic Pizza Dough— semolina variation (page 11), at room temperature

½ cup grated aged Monterey Jack cheese

2 tablespoons coarsely chopped fresh cilantro

1. Arrange one rack on the bottom rung of the oven. Preheat the oven to 500°F. Spray a large baking sheet with nonstick spray.

2. Heat a large nonstick skillet over medium-high heat. Swirl in the oil, then add the bell peppers, onion, jalapeño peppers, and salt. Cook, stirring frequently, until softened, about 10 minutes. Stir in the garlic and pepper sauce; cook 1 minute. Stir in the tomato, then remove the skillet from the heat.

3. Sprinkle a work surface lightly with flour. Turn the dough onto the surface; knead lightly. Divide the dough in half. With a lightly floured rolling pin, roll each half into a 4 × 16-inch oval. Transfer the ovals to the baking sheet. Evenly spread the pepper mixture on the ovals almost to the edges. Sprinkle with the cheese. Bake on the bottom rack of the oven until the crusts are golden at the edges, 10–12 minutes.

4. Slide one pizza onto a large cutting board. Sprinkle with 1 tablespoon of the cilantro. Using a pizza wheel or sharp knife, make cuts crosswise, alternating the angle, to make 10 wedges. Repeat with the remaining pizza, making a total of 20 wedges.

Per serving (2 wedges): 154 Cal, 4 g Fat, 1 g Sat Fat, 5 mg Chol, 277 mg Sod, 25 g Carb, 2 g Fib, 5 g Prot, 53 mg Calc. **_POINTS: 3._**

 tip The bell pepper mixture is sautéed first to remove excess moisture and to intensify the sweet flavor of the peppers. You can do this up to four hours ahead.

Spicy Stromboli Slices

Makes 24 servings

These savory olive-and-cheese spirals make a great party appetizer. They can be made ahead and kept in the freezer for up to two months. To reheat, bake in a 350°F oven for 10 to 15 minutes.

½ cup chopped fresh basil

¼ cup grated Parmesan cheese

6 pitted kalamata olives, finely chopped

6 medium pimiento-stuffed green olives, finely chopped

4 oil-packed sun-dried tomatoes, rinsed, patted dry, and finely chopped

2 garlic cloves, minced

¼ teaspoon dried oregano

¼ teaspoon crushed red pepper

½ recipe (about 1 pound) Basic Pizza Dough (page 10), at room temperature

½ cup shredded provolone cheese

1. Preheat the oven to 425°F. Spray a baking sheet with nonstick spray.

2. Combine the basil, Parmesan cheese, kalamata and green olives, tomatoes, garlic, oregano, and crushed red pepper in a small bowl; set aside.

3. Sprinkle a work surface lightly with flour. Turn the dough onto the surface; knead lightly. Cut the dough in half and with a lightly floured rolling pin, roll one half into an 8 × 12-inch rectangle. Sprinkle with half of the basil mixture, up to ½ inch from the edges. Sprinkle with half of the provolone cheese. Brush one long edge lightly with water. Roll up the dough from the unbrushed long side. Pinch the seam to seal. Place the loaf, seam-side down, on the baking sheet. Pinch the ends to seal and tuck under.

4. Repeat with the remaining dough and filling. Make 5 shallow lengthwise slashes in the top of each loaf. Bake until golden, about 20 minutes. Let cool on a rack 5 minutes. Transfer to a cutting board, then cut each loaf into 24 (½-inch) slices, making a total of 48 slices. Serve warm or at room temperature.

Per serving (2 slices): 64 Cal, 2 g Fat, 1 g Sat Fat, 3 mg Chol, 153 mg Sod, 9 g Carb, 0 g Fib, 2 g Prot, 38 mg Calc. *POINTS: 1.*

Mini Calzones with Goat Cheese and Figs

Makes 12 servings

Creamy goat cheese, intense prosciutto, sweet figs, leeks, and garlic make a sophisticated, luscious filling for these little turnovers. Use the tender white and pale green part of the leek only and, if you prefer, chop it fine instead of slicing it.

1 small leek, halved lengthwise, then thinly sliced (about 1½ cups)

¼ cup water

1 large garlic clove, minced

1½ ounces goat cheese

¼ cup grated Parmesan cheese

1 (1-ounce) slice prosciutto, finely chopped

2 dried Calimyrna figs, finely chopped

½ teaspoon minced fresh rosemary, or ⅛ teaspoon dried, crumbled

⅛ teaspoon salt

1 (6.5-ounce) package pizza crust dry mix

1. Combine the leek and water in a medium skillet; bring to a boil. Reduce the heat and simmer, covered, until soft and the water evaporates, about 8 minutes. Stir in the garlic, then remove the skillet from the heat; let cool.

2. Combine the leek mixture, goat cheese, 3 tablespoons of the Parmesan cheese, the prosciutto, figs, rosemary, and salt in a bowl; stir with a fork until well blended.

3. Preheat the oven to 450°F. Spray a large baking sheet with nonstick spray.

4. Prepare the pizza crust mix according to package directions. Sprinkle a work surface lightly with flour. Turn the dough onto the surface; knead lightly. With a lightly floured rolling pin, roll into a 12-inch square. Cut the dough into 36 squares. Place a level measuring teaspoon of filling in the center of each square. Brush one side of each square lightly with water. Fold the moistened side of the dough over the filling, pressing the edges firmly to seal and flouring fingers if necessary. You will have a total of 36 calzones.

5. Place the calzones on the baking sheet, 1 inch apart. With the tip of a sharp knife, make a small slit in the top of each calzone. Brush the calzones lightly with water, then sprinkle with the remaining 1 tablespoon Parmesan cheese. Bake until golden brown, 10–12 minutes.

Per serving (3 calzones): 93 Cal, 2 g Fat, 1 g Sat Fat, 6 mg Chol, 231 mg Sod, 14 g Carb, 1 g Fib, 4 g Prot, 59 mg Calc. *POINTS: 2.*

 tip There are several techniques for cleaning leeks. Here's one simple version: Slice the leeks first, then rinse thoroughly in a colander to remove any sand.

Plum Tomato Galette

Makes 12 servings

This pretty phyllo-pastry tart (*galette* is the French name for tart) is assembled with very little effort. Phyllo dough may sound daunting, but it is truly one of the easiest pastries to use. Try to find Italian fontina cheese—it has great flavor and creamy texture.

4 (12 × 17-inch) sheets phyllo dough, thawed according to package directions

¼ cup grated Parmesan cheese

½ cup shredded fontina cheese

2 plum tomatoes, very thinly sliced

½ teaspoon salt-free garlic-herb seasoning blend

3 tablespoons chopped red onion

6 pitted black olives, chopped

4 large fresh basil leaves

1. Preheat the oven to 375°F. Stack the sheets of phyllo dough on a cutting board; cut in half crosswise. As you work, keep the phyllo covered with plastic wrap to keep it from drying out.
2. Place one piece of phyllo on a nonstick baking sheet. Sprinkle evenly with 1½ teaspoons of the Parmesan cheese. Repeat the layering until all of the phyllo and Parmesan cheese have been used. Sprinkle the top layer with half of the fontina cheese. Arrange the tomato slices on top and sprinkle with the garlic-herb blend, red onion, olives, and the remaining fontina cheese.
3. Bake the galette until the phyllo is browned and crisp, about 25 minutes. Stack the basil leaves and cut into thin strips; sprinkle over the top of the galette. Slide the galette onto a cutting board and cut into 24 rectangles.

Per serving (2 pieces): 47 Cal, 2 g Fat, 1 g Sat Fat, 6 mg Chol, 104 mg Sod, 4 g Carb, 0 g Fib, 2 g Prot, 65 mg Calc. *POINTS: 1.*

 tip Salt-free seasoning blends are a great way to add lots of flavor without adding salt. They are widely available in large supermarkets.

**Pizza Twists with
Tomato Dipping Sauce**

Pizza Twists with Tomato Dipping Sauce

Makes 16 servings

To keep this easy, we use store-bought pizza dough and bottled pizza sauce. Store-bought dough doesn't always roll out as easily as homemade, so it's important to let it come to room temperature for about an hour before using. Smooth rather than chunky sauce works best here.

1 pound refrigerated pizza dough, at room temperature

½ cup bottled pizza sauce

1 teaspoon dried Italian seasoning

1 ounce reduced-fat sliced pepperoni, finely chopped

½ cup grated Romano cheese

1. Arrange one rack on the top rung of the oven. Preheat the oven to 425°F. Spray 2 large baking sheets with nonstick spray.

2. Sprinkle a work surface lightly with flour. Turn the dough onto the surface; knead lightly. With a lightly floured rolling pin, roll into a 12-inch square. Brush with 2 tablespoons of the pizza sauce. Sprinkle with the Italian seasoning, pepperoni, and cheese. Press the cheese lightly so it sticks to the dough. Cut the dough in half. Cut each half crosswise into 16 strips. Twist the strips and place 1 inch apart on the baking sheets, pressing the ends lightly to prevent them from untwisting. Cover loosely with plastic wrap and let rest 15 minutes.

3. Bake one sheet at a time, on the top shelf of the oven, until golden brown, 10–12 minutes. Transfer the twists to a rack to cool. Heat the remaining pizza sauce and serve for dipping.

Per serving (2 twists and about 1 teaspoon sauce): 94 Cal, 3 g Fat, 1 g Sat Fat, 3 mg Chol, 200 mg Sod, 15 g Carb, 1 g Fib, 3 g Prot, 22 mg Calc. *POINTS: 2.*

 tip A mini food processor works really well for chopping the pepperoni.

Three-Cheese and Roasted-Garlic Pizza Strips

Makes 8 servings

This pizza is packed with intense flavors of the Mediterranean—roasted garlic, goat cheese, tomatoes, oregano, and capers. To save time on serving day, roast the garlic cloves a day ahead. To save peeling time, use peeled whole garlic cloves from a jar.

20 medium garlic cloves, peeled

6 sun-dried tomatoes (not oil-packed)

1 (8-ounce) package individual prebaked pizza crusts (two 6-inch crusts)

2 teaspoons capers, drained

2 ounces reduced-fat goat cheese

⅓ cup shredded part-skim mozzarella cheese

¼ teaspoon dried oregano

1 tablespoon shredded Parmesan cheese

1. Preheat the oven to 350°F. Wrap the garlic cloves in foil and bake until soft, about 45 minutes. Let cool.

2. Combine the sun-dried tomatoes with enough boiling water to cover in a small bowl. Let stand until softened, about 15 minutes. Drain the tomatoes, then cut into thin strips.

3. Increase the oven temperature to 450°F. Place the pizza crusts on a baking sheet. Top evenly with the garlic cloves, tomato strips, and capers. Crumble the goat cheese into small pieces and sprinkle on top. Sprinkle with the mozzarella cheese, oregano, and Parmesan cheese. Bake until hot and the crusts are crisp, 10–12 minutes. Place the pizzas on a cutting board. Cut each pizza into 4 strips, then cut the strips in half, making a total of 16 strips.

Per serving (2 strips): 133 Cal, 4 g Fat, 2 g Sat Fat, 9 mg Chol, 321 mg Sod, 20 g Carb, 1 g Fib, 6 g Prot, 103 mg Calc. **POINTS: 3.**

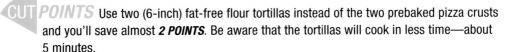

CUT POINTS Use two (6-inch) fat-free flour tortillas instead of the two prebaked pizza crusts and you'll save almost **2 POINTS**. Be aware that the tortillas will cook in less time—about 5 minutes.

Greek Island Pitzas

Makes 16 servingss

Feta cheese is available in several wonderful flavors, and it conveniently comes already crumbled. If you can't find the basil-tomato flavor, try another variety, or plain feta cheese. Serve these wedges as tasty appetizer bites. You can also dish up a whole pitza for a satisfying lunch (it will cost you a mere *4 POINTS* for one).

8 frozen artichoke hearts, thawed and coarsely chopped

1 small zucchini, coarsely shredded

1 large garlic clove, minced

¼ teaspoon dried oregano

4 (6-inch) whole-wheat pita breads

12 cherry tomatoes, halved

6 large kalamata olives, pitted and sliced

¼ cup crumbled basil-tomato feta cheese

¼ cup shredded part-skim mozzarella cheese

1 scallion, thinly sliced

1. Preheat the oven to 425°F. Spray a nonstick skillet with nonstick spray and set over medium-high heat. Add the artichoke hearts, zucchini, garlic, and oregano. Cook, stirring frequently, until the zucchini is tender, about 2 minutes.

2. Place the pita breads on a baking sheet. Evenly spread the zucchini mixture on the pitas almost to the edge. Top with the cherry tomatoes and olives; sprinkle with the feta and mozzarella cheeses. Bake until heated through and the cheeses melt, about 10 minutes. Sprinkle with the scallion, then cut each pita into 4 wedges.

Per serving (1 wedge): 60 Cal, 1 g Fat, 1 g Sat Fat, 3 mg Chol, 137 mg Sod, 10 g Carb, 2 g Fib, 3 g Prot, 37 mg Calc. *POINTS: 1.*

Summer Garden Pizzettes

Makes 8 servings

Fresh flavors from seasonal vegetables burst from these mini pizzas. A little cheese and fresh basil complement the summer combination of fresh corn, onion, zucchini, and ripe tomato. Use small flour or corn tortillas instead of the English muffins, if you prefer.

1 teaspoon olive oil
1 small onion, chopped
1 small zucchini, finely diced
¼ teaspoon salt
½ cup fresh corn kernels
1 ripe medium tomato, diced
4 English muffins, split
¾ cup shredded reduced-fat Monterey Jack cheese
2 tablespoons grated Parmesan cheese
8 fresh basil leaves, thinly sliced

1. Preheat the oven to 450°F.
2. Heat a large nonstick skillet over medium-high heat. Swirl in the oil, then add the onion. Cook, stirring occasionally, until softened and just beginning to brown, about 2 minutes. Add the zucchini and salt, reduce the heat to medium, and cook, stirring occasionally, until the zucchini is tender, about 3 minutes. Stir in the corn and cook 1 minute. Stir in the tomato, then remove from the heat.
3. Arrange the English muffins, cut-side up, on a baking sheet. Sprinkle evenly with half of the Monterey Jack cheese and half of the Parmesan cheese. Spoon on the vegetable mixture, then sprinkle with the remaining Monterey Jack and Parmesan cheeses. Bake until the muffins are heated through and the cheese melts, 8–10 minutes. Sprinkle evenly with the basil, then let stand 5 minutes. With a sharp knife, cut each muffin into quarters, making a total of 32 wedges.

Per serving (4 wedges): 125 Cal, 3 g Fat, 2 g Sat Fat, 7 mg Chol, 292 mg Sod, 17 g Carb, 2 g Fib, 6 g Prot, 154 mg Calc. *POINTS: 2.*

 tip There's nothing like fresh corn from the cob for great flavor and texture. To cut the kernels from the cob, stand the ear of shucked corn on a cutting board, and using a sharp knife, cut the kernels down and away from the ear of corn. One ear of corn will yield ½ cup kernels.

Tomato Bruschetta Slices

Makes 8 servings

Fully ripe, juicy tomatoes are what make this bruschetta special, so this appetizer is best when either ripe tomatoes are available in your market or you have a few days to let them ripen on a counter. To speed up the ripening process, place them in a paper bag with an apple. Whatever you do, don't refrigerate tomatoes—cold damages their texture and flavor. When spooning the tomato mixture over the toasted bread, make sure to include the flavorful juices.

4 ripe tomatoes, chopped
12 large fresh basil leaves, thinly sliced
2 large garlic cloves, minced
⅛ teaspoon salt
⅓ cup grated Romano cheese
¼ (8-ounce,10-inch) French bread, halved horizontally

1. Preheat the oven to 400°F. Combine the tomatoes, the basil, ¼ teaspoon of the garlic, and the salt in a medium bowl. Combine the remaining garlic and the cheese in a small bowl.

2. Arrange the French bread halves cut-side up on a baking sheet. Sprinkle evenly with the cheese mixture. Bake until golden brown, 10–12 minutes. Place the bread on a cutting board and cut each half into 4 pieces. Spoon the tomato mixture on the warm bread pieces. Serve at once.

Per serving (1 piece): 67 Cal, 2 g Fat, 1 g Sat Fat, 4 mg Chol, 163 mg Sod, 10 g Carb, 1 g Fib, 3 g Prot, 47 mg Calc. *POINTS: 1.*

 tip For zippier flavor, add 1 teaspoon aged balsamic vinegar to the tomato mixture.

Hearty Pizzas

Pies for Big Appetites

California Pizzettes with Smoked Chicken and Sun-Dried Tomato Pesto

Makes 6 servings

Colorful and easy to put together, these mini pizzas use some of the delicious staples of California cuisine—fresh herbs and vegetables, sun-dried tomatoes, and flavorful cheeses. If you own a mini food processor, use it instead of the regular-sized processor to make the pesto in this recipe.

4 large sun-dried tomatoes (not oil-packed)
½ cup basil leaves
2 tablespoons grated Parmesan cheese
1 large garlic clove
1 teaspoon olive oil
⅛ teaspoon crushed red pepper
⅛ teaspoon salt
1 large yellow bell pepper, seeded and diced
1 leek, halved lengthwise, then sliced
4 ounces skinless smoked chicken or turkey, diced
6 (7-inch) whole-wheat flour tortillas
5 plum tomatoes, sliced
2 ounces garlic-herb-coated goat cheese, crumbled
¾ cup shredded Monterey Jack cheese
2 tablespoons chopped walnuts

1. Combine the sun-dried tomatoes with enough boiling water to cover in a small bowl; let stand until softened, about 15 minutes. Remove the tomatoes from the water and reserve 3 tablespoons of the soaking water.

2. To make the sun-dried tomato pesto, combine 2 tablespoons of the soaking water, the sun-dried tomatoes, basil, Parmesan cheese, garlic, oil, crushed red pepper, and salt in a food processor and pulse until a paste is formed, adding the remaining 1 tablespoon soaking water if necessary.

3. Preheat the oven to 450°F. Spray 2 large baking sheets with nonstick spray.

4. Spray a large nonstick skillet with nonstick spray; set over medium heat. Add the bell pepper and leek. Cook, covered, stirring occasionally, until the vegetables soften, about 5 minutes. Uncover and cook to evaporate any moisture, about 1 minute. Remove from the heat and stir in the chicken.

5. Place the tortillas on the baking sheets. Spread the pesto on the tortillas to 1 inch from the edges. Top with the chicken mixture, then the tomato slices. Sprinkle with the goat cheese, then the Monterey Jack cheese and walnuts. Bake one sheet at a time, until the tortillas are crisp and browned at the edges, about 10 minutes.

Per serving (1 pizette): 226 Cal, 11 g Fat, 5 g Sat Fat, 31 mg Chol, 701 mg Sod, 21 g Carb, 4 g Fib, 13 g Prot, 217 mg Calc. **POINTS: 5.**

Sicilian Sausage-Stuffed Pizza

Makes 8 servings

This rustic pizza is similar to what Sicilians call a *sfincione*—a two-crust pie believed to have been made by Sicilian peasant farmers long before anyone in the rest of Italy thought of making pizza. It's good hot or at room temperature. You can substitute turkey kielbasa for the chicken sausage if you like.

½ pound fully cooked smoked chicken sausage, coarsely chopped

1 pound fresh cremini or white button mushrooms, sliced

1 medium onion, chopped

1 large garlic clove, minced

½ cup shredded part-skim mozzarella cheese

¼ cup part-skim ricotta cheese

¼ cup grated Romano or Parmesan cheese

½ recipe (about 1 pound) Basic Pizza Dough (page 10), at room temperature

1. Preheat the oven to 500°F.
2. Spray a large nonstick skillet with nonstick spray and set over medium-high heat. Add the sausage and cook until lightly browned, about 5 minutes; transfer to a bowl. Add the mushrooms and onion to the skillet. Cook, stirring occasionally, until the mushrooms give off liquid, it evaporates, and the mushrooms are golden, about 10 minutes. Stir in the garlic and cook 1 minute. Add the mushroom mixture to the sausage; let cool. Stir in the mozzarella, ricotta, and Romano cheeses.
3. Sprinkle a work surface lightly with flour. Turn the dough onto the surface; knead lightly. Cut the dough in half. With a lightly floured rolling pin, roll one half into a thin 12-inch circle. Transfer the circle of dough to a nonstick pizza pan or large baking sheet, gently pulling the dough back to a 12-inch circle. Spread the filling onto the dough, to ¾ inch from the edge. Brush around the outer edge with water.
4. Roll the remaining dough into a 12-inch circle and place on top of the filling. Press the edges together to seal, then crimp the edges. Cut 5 (2-inch) slits in the top of the dough. Bake until the crust is golden, about 15 minutes. Let cool 5–10 minutes and serve hot, or let the pie cool on a rack and serve at room temperature.

Per serving (⅛ of pizza): 238 Cal, 7 g Fat, 3 g Sat Fat, 25 mg Chol, 552 mg Sod, 31 g Carb, 2 g Fib, 13 g Prot, 112 mg Calc. **_POINTS: 5._**

Chicago Pizza with Ham, Cheese, and Roasted Peppers

Chicago Pizza with Ham, Cheese, and Roasted Peppers

Makes 6 servings

Ham coated with paprika and hot pepper, sometimes called cappy or capicola ham, adds rich flavor to this deep-dish pizza, but any kind of thinly sliced smoked ham would be fine. Roasting the bell peppers from scratch gives a smoky flavor to the pizza. To save time, you could substitute jarred roasted peppers, and simply rinse and pat dry before cutting them into strips.

2 red bell peppers

1 (14-ounce) can diced tomatoes in juice, drained

2 garlic cloves, minced

½ teaspoon dried oregano

⅛ teaspoon crushed red pepper

2 tablespoons grated Parmesan cheese

6 oil-cured black olives, pitted and chopped

½ recipe (about 1 pound) Basic Pizza Dough— semolina variation (page 11), at room temperature

1 cup shredded part-skim mozzarella cheese

4 ounces thinly sliced cappy ham, coarsely chopped

6 large basil leaves

1. Preheat the broiler. Line a baking sheet with foil; place the bell peppers on the baking sheet. Broil 5 inches from the heat, turning frequently with tongs, until lightly charred, about 10 minutes. Wrap the bell peppers in the foil and let steam for 10 minutes. When cool enough to handle, peel, discard seeds, and cut into 1-inch strips.

2. Arrange one rack on the bottom rung of the oven. Preheat the oven to 500°F.

3. Combine the tomatoes, garlic, oregano, and crushed red pepper in a medium nonstick skillet; bring to a boil. Reduce the heat and simmer, uncovered, 5 minutes. Let cool. Stir in the Parmesan cheese and olives.

4. Spray a 10-inch cast-iron or other ovenproof skillet with nonstick spray.

5. Sprinkle a work surface lightly with flour. Turn the dough onto the surface; knead lightly. With a lightly floured rolling pin, roll into a 13-inch circle. Transfer the circle of dough to the skillet, gently pulling the dough up the sides of the skillet. Spoon the tomato mixture onto the dough. Sprinkle with half of the mozzarella cheese. Top with the roasted bell pepper strips and ham. Bake on the bottom rack of the oven 10 minutes. Sprinkle with the remaining mozzarella cheese and bake until the crust is browned, 8–10 minutes. Let cool 5 minutes. Thinly slice the basil and sprinkle over the top, just before serving.

Per serving (⅙ of pizza): 297 Cal, 8 g Fat, 3 g Sat Fat, 21 mg Chol, 815 mg Sod, 41 g Carb, 3 g Fib, 16 g Prot, 202 mg Calc. **POINTS: 6.**

Turkey Alfredo-Saltimbocca Pizza with Asparagus

Makes 4 servings

This pizza combines two Italian favorites—creamy Alfredo sauce and the classic Roman saltimbocca, made with veal or turkey, prosciutto, and sage. Pencil-thin asparagus stalks are needed here, since thicker asparagus won't cook through in the short time it takes to cook the pizza. Find prepared Alfredo sauce in the refrigerator section of the supermarket.

1 (6.5-ounce) package pizza crust dry mix
⅓ cup prepared light Alfredo sauce
1 (4-ounce) thick slice roast skinless turkey breast, cut into thin strips
1½ ounces part-skim mozzarella cheese, cut into thin strips
24 pencil-thin asparagus stalks, trimmed to 5-inch lengths
3 tablespoons grated Parmesan cheese
1 small garlic clove, minced
1 tablespoon chopped flat-leaf parsley
1½ teaspoons minced fresh sage
½ teaspoon grated lemon zest
1 paper-thin slice prosciutto, cut into thin strips

1. Preheat the oven to 450°F. Spray a pizza pan or baking sheet with nonstick spray.

2. Prepare the pizza crust mix according to package directions. Sprinkle a work surface lightly with flour. Turn the dough onto the surface; knead lightly. With a lightly floured rolling pin, roll into a 12-inch circle. Transfer the circle of dough to the pizza pan, gently pulling the dough back to a 12-inch circle. Spread the Alfredo sauce onto the dough, to 1 inch from the edge. Arrange the turkey, mozzarella cheese, and asparagus, tip ends out, in a pinwheel pattern on the sauce.

3. Bake until the crust is golden at the edges, 12–14 minutes. Meanwhile, combine the Parmesan cheese, garlic, parsley, sage, and lemon zest in a small bowl. Arrange the prosciutto on the pizza, then sprinkle with the Parmesan cheese mixture. Bake until the Parmesan cheese melts slightly, about 1 minute.

Per serving (¼ of pizza): 338 Cal, 11 g Fat, 5 g Sat Fat, 41 mg Chol, 678 mg Sod, 36 g Carb, 3 g Fib, 23 g Prot, 242 mg Calc. **POINTS: 7.**

 Save the tender portion of the trimmed asparagus stalks for a salad.

Sausage and Pepperoni Biscuit-Crust Pizza

Makes 6 servings

Meat lovers will enjoy this pizza, which combines a generous amount of chicken sausage and pepperoni. We keep the *POINTS* in line by using just a sprinkling of cheese on top, for flavor, and turkey pepperoni, a leaner version than regular. It comes in small, thin, ready-to-eat slices (about 100 slices to a 6-ounce package). Reduced-fat baking mix makes a pizza dough that is especially easy to prepare, and prebaking helps reduce sogginess.

2 green bell peppers, seeded and sliced into rings

1 medium onion, thinly sliced

¼ cup water

3 garlic cloves, minced

⅛ teaspoon crushed red pepper (optional)

2 cups reduced-fat baking mix

⅔ cup fat-free milk

1 cup Basic Tomato Sauce (page 12)

½ pound fully cooked hot Italian chicken sausage, cut into ½-inch-thick slices

16 slices (1-ounce) reduced-fat turkey pepperoni

3 tablespoons grated Parmesan cheese

1. Arrange one rack on the bottom rung of the oven. Preheat the oven to 450°F. Spray a baking sheet with nonstick spray.

2. Combine the bell peppers, onion, water, garlic, and crushed red pepper, if using, in a large nonstick skillet; bring to a boil. Reduce the heat and simmer, stirring occasionally, until the vegetables are tender and all of the water evaporates, about 12 minutes.

3. Combine the baking mix and milk in a small bowl. Stir with a fork until a soft dough forms; let stand 5 minutes. Sprinkle a work surface lightly with flour. Turn the dough onto the surface; knead lightly. With a lightly floured rolling pin, roll into a 13-inch circle. Transfer the circle of dough to the baking sheet and prick all over with a fork. Bake on the bottom rack of the oven until the crust is lightly browned, about 5 minutes.

4. Spread the tomato sauce over the crust to ½ inch from the edge. Spoon on the vegetable mixture. Arrange the sausage and pepperoni slices on top, then sprinkle with the cheese. Bake until the crust is golden at the edges, 10–12 minutes.

Per serving (⅙ of pizza): 269 Cal, 8 g Fat, 2 g Sat Fat, 27 mg Chol, 1137 mg Sod, 35 g Carb, 2 g Fib, 14 g Prot, 131 mg Calc. *POINTS: 6.*

Spicy Pork Taco Pizzas

Spicy Pork Taco Pizzas

Makes 6 servings

Here is a delightful fusion of a traditional Italian pizza crust with a topping that's pure Mexican. The peasant crust, called a *piadina*, is made with baking powder instead of yeast, and the dough is cooked in a skillet instead of in the oven, so the crust stays soft and can be folded in half. Taco cheese is a mixture of taco seasoning, Monterey Jack and colby or cheddar cheese. For spicier tacos, use a medium or hot salsa and add chopped pickled jalapeño peppers to the sour cream sauce.

1⅓ cups all-purpose flour
⅓ cup cornmeal
½ teaspoon baking powder
½ teaspoon salt
½ cup + 1 tablespoon warm water (105-115°F)
1½ teaspoons olive oil
3 tablespoons fat-free sour cream
1½ tablespoons fresh lime juice
1 tablespoon chopped fresh cilantro
½ pound pork tenderloin, trimmed of all visible fat and cut into thin strips
¾ teaspoon ground cumin
½ teaspoon chili powder
⅛ teaspoon cayenne
1 cup frozen corn, thawed
½ cup mild thick-and-chunky salsa
¾ cup shredded taco cheese
3 cups shredded lettuce

1. Preheat the oven to 250°F. Combine the flour, cornmeal, baking powder, and salt in a food processor. With the machine running, add the water and oil. Pulse until the dough forms a ball, about 1 minute. Turn the dough onto a lightly floured surface and knead until smooth. Cover with plastic wrap and let rest 15 minutes.
2. Meanwhile, combine the sour cream, lime juice, and cilantro in a small bowl; whisk to blend and set aside. Toss the pork, cumin, chili powder, and cayenne in a bowl; set aside.
3. Divide the dough into 6 pieces. Sprinkle a work surface lightly with flour. With a floured rolling pin, roll each piece of dough into a 5½-inch circle. Spray a large nonstick skillet with nonstick spray and set over medium-high heat. Add one circle; cook until lightly browned, 30–60 seconds on each side. Transfer the circle to a large nonstick baking sheet. Repeat with the remaining 5 dough circles. Place in the oven to keep warm.
4. Return the skillet to the heat. Add the pork mixture and corn; stir-fry until the pork is cooked through, 2–3 minutes. Stir in the salsa.
5. To assemble, spoon the pork mixture onto the 6 crusts to cover half, sprinkle evenly with the cheese and lettuce, then drizzle each with a scant tablespoon of the sour cream mixture. Fold and eat like a taco.

Per serving (1 taco): 282 Cal, 8 g Fat, 4 g Sat Fat, 39 mg Chol, 411 mg Sod, 35 g Carb, 3 g Fib, 17 g Prot, 140 mg Calc. *POINTS: 6.*

Thai Pork Satay Pizza

Makes 6 servings

As you look at the ingredient list, your first reaction might be that this is one of those wacky pizzas (remember Hawaiian pizzas?). But the combination of pork, pineapple, and a peanut-hoisin sauce really tastes great. Substitute pork tenderloin or skinless boneless chicken breasts for the pork cutlets, if you like. If pineapple tidbits in juice are unavailable, use chunks and cut them in half.

¼ cup canned tomato sauce

2 tablespoons bottled peanut sauce

2 tablespoons bottled hoisin sauce

1 (10-ounce) thin prebaked pizza crust

½ cup shredded part-skim mozzarella cheese

¾ cup shredded carrot

1 (8-ounce) can pineapple tidbits in juice, drained and patted dry

½ pound pork loin cutlets, trimmed of all visible fat, cut into thin strips

½ cup fresh bean sprouts

1 scallion, thinly sliced

2 tablespoons chopped fresh cilantro

1½ tablespoons unsalted dry-roasted peanuts, chopped

1. Preheat the oven to 450°F. Combine the tomato sauce, peanut sauce, and hoisin sauce in a small bowl. Set aside 2 tablespoons of the sauce mixture.

2. Spread the remaining sauce mixture on the pizza crust and place the crust on a nonstick pizza pan or baking sheet. Sprinkle with half of the cheese, then the carrot, pineapple, and remaining cheese. Bake until heated through and the cheese melts, 10–12 minutes.

3. Meanwhile, spray a large nonstick skillet with nonstick spray and set over medium-high heat. Add the pork and stir-fry until just cooked through, about 2 minutes. Stir in 1 tablespoon of the reserved sauce and remove the skillet from the heat.

4. Spoon the pork onto the pizza, then sprinkle with the bean sprouts. Drizzle with the remaining 1 tablespoon reserved sauce, then sprinkle with the scallion, cilantro, and peanuts.

Per serving (⅙ of pizza): 306 Cal, 12 g Fat, 3 g Sat Fat, 29 mg Chol, 357 mg Sod, 33 g Carb, 3 g Fib, 17 g Prot, 119 mg Calc. **POINTS: 7.**

 tip To save time, buy a bag of shredded carrots from the produce section of the supermarket. Also, you can stack the pork cutlets on top of one another, then slice them crosswise into thin strips.

Sausage and Broccoli Calzones

Makes 6 servings

Since most of the ingredients for these tasty calzones are easily kept on hand in the refrigerator or freezer, this is a recipe that can take less time than ordering out. To prevent the calzones from becoming soggy, place the thawed broccoli between layers of paper towels and press gently to remove any excess moisture. Serve with a favorite bottled pizza sauce if you like.

½ pound hot or sweet Italian turkey sausage, casings removed

1 (10-ounce) box frozen chopped broccoli, thawed and patted dry

1 large garlic clove, minced

¼ teaspoon crushed red pepper

½ cup shredded sharp provolone cheese

⅓ cup fat-free ricotta cheese

1 (10-ounce) tube refrigerated pizza dough

1. Preheat the oven to 425°F. Spray a large baking sheet with nonstick spray.
2. Spray a large nonstick skillet with nonstick spray and set over medium-high heat. Add the sausage, breaking it up into small pieces with a spoon, and cook until browned and cooked through, about 6 minutes. Add the broccoli, garlic, and crushed red pepper. Cook, stirring, about 1 minute. Transfer the mixture to a bowl and let cool, about 10 minutes. Add the provolone and ricotta cheeses; stir until well blended.
3. Sprinkle a work surface lightly with flour. Unroll the pizza dough onto the surface. With a lightly floured rolling pin, roll the dough into an 11 × 16-inch rectangle. Cut the rectangle into 6 squares.
4. Spoon the sausage mixture evenly onto the squares, using about ½ cup for each, and covering half of the dough in a rectangular mound, to ½ inch from the edges. Fold the dough over the filling and press the edges firmly to seal. Place the calzones on the baking sheet. Make 3 slashes in the top of each calzone. Bake until the crust is golden, about 12 minutes.

Per serving (1 calzone): 264 Cal, 10 g Fat, 3 g Sat Fat, 36 mg Chol, 700 mg Sod, 27 g Carb, 2 g Fib, 17 g Prot, 127 mg Calc. **POINTS: 6.**

CUT POINTS Substitute ¼ cup shredded reduced-fat cheese (provolone, cheddar, or mozzarella) for the regular provolone cheese and save almost a **POINT** per serving.

Chicken Pizza Française

Makes 6 servings

A few "French" ingredients combine here to make an especially tasty pizza. If leeks are available, substitute one large leek for the onions. Herbes de Provence is a delightful mixture of dried herbs used in Provence and other parts of southern France. The mixture varies, but usually contains a combination of thyme, rosemary, lavender, basil, marjoram, sage, savory, fennel, and oregano.

3 (4-ounce) skinless boneless chicken breasts

2 large garlic cloves, minced

¼ teaspoon dried herbes de Provence or thyme

¼ teaspoon freshly ground pepper

3 medium onions, sliced

5 tablespoons water

1 (9-ounce) bag baby spinach

1 (10-ounce) thin prebaked pizza crust

2 tablespoons Dijon mustard

2 tablespoons reduced-fat mayonnaise

½ cup shredded Gruyère cheese

1. Preheat the oven to 450°F.

2. Place the chicken breasts on a plate; sprinkle both sides with half of the garlic, the herbes de Provence, and pepper. Spray a large nonstick skillet with nonstick spray and set over medium-high heat. Add the chicken and cook until lightly browned and just cooked through, about 3 minutes on each side. Transfer to a plate.

3. Add the onions and 4 tablespoons of the water to the skillet; bring to a boil. Reduce the heat and cook, stirring occasionally, until golden, 15–20 minutes. Add the remaining garlic, remaining 1 tablespoon water, and half of the spinach to the skillet. Increase the heat to medium-high and cook, stirring constantly, until the spinach wilts. Add the remaining spinach and cook until wilted.

4. Place the pizza crust on a nonstick pizza pan or baking sheet. Whisk the mustard and mayonnaise in a small bowl and spread over the crust. Spoon on the onion-spinach mixture, spreading to cover the crust. Slice the chicken breasts on the diagonal into long thin strips; arrange over the onion-spinach mixture. Sprinkle with the cheese. Bake until heated through and the cheese melts, about 12 minutes.

Per serving (⅙ of pizza): 285 Cal, 9 g Fat, 3 g Sat Fat, 41 mg Chol, 410 mg Sod, 31 g Carb, 3 g Fib, 20 g Prot, 159 mg Calc. *POINTS: 6.*

Chicken Pizza Francaise

Pizza Bolognese

Makes 8 servings

This classic beef pasta sauce is a favorite with spaghetti, and it's great as a topping for pizza. To make it a quick meal, we spoon the topping on Italian bread, but for a more traditional pizza, it's also terrific on a thin prebaked pizza crust.

1 small onion, finely chopped
1 small carrot, finely chopped
1 celery stalk, finely chopped
½ pound fresh cremini mushrooms, quartered
¾ pound lean ground beef (10% or less fat)
¾ cup fat-free bottled pasta sauce
¼ cup low-fat (1%) milk
1 (12-ounce) loaf Italian bread, halved horizontally
4 plum tomatoes, sliced
½ cup shredded Italian cheese blend

1. Preheat the oven to 400°F.
2. Spray a large nonstick skillet with nonstick spray and set over medium heat. Add the onion, carrot, celery, and mushrooms and cook, stirring frequently, until the vegetables soften and the mushrooms exude liquid, about 6 minutes.
3. Increase the heat to medium-high and stir in the beef. Cook, stirring frequently to break up the beef, until browned, about 5 minutes. Stir in the pasta sauce and milk; bring to a boil. Reduce the heat and simmer to blend the flavors, about 5 minutes.
4. Place the bread, cut-side up, on a nonstick baking sheet. Spoon the meat sauce onto the bread, spreading it evenly. Arrange the tomatoes on top. Bake until heated through and the bread is browned at the edges, about 10 minutes. Sprinkle evenly with the cheese and bake until the cheese melts, about 5 minutes. Cut each piece of bread into fourths, making a total of 8 pieces.

Per serving (1 piece): 233 Cal, 7 g Fat, 3 g Sat Fat, 30 mg Chol, 443 mg Sod, 28 g Carb, 3 g Fib, 16 g Prot, 108 mg Calc. *POINTS: 5.*

 tip Shredded cheese blends can save you lots of time while providing a wonderful combination of creamy and sharp flavors. Italian cheese blend is a mixture of mozzarella, provolone, Romano, and Parmesan cheeses.

Chicken Caesar-Salad Pitzas

Makes 4 servings

Here's a favorite salad turned into hearty individual pizzas. For a change of pace, use four 6-inch flour tortillas instead of the two pita breads and bake them for only 4 to 6 minutes.

4 (4-ounce) skinless boneless chicken breasts

2 large garlic cloves, minced

¼ teaspoon salt

⅛ teaspoon freshly ground pepper

1 large zucchini, cut lengthwise into ¼-inch-thick slices

¼ cup finely shredded Parmesan cheese

2 (6-inch) pita breads, halved horizontally

3 tablespoons reduced-fat creamy Caesar dressing

1 tablespoon fresh lemon juice

1 teaspoon Dijon mustard

1 large heart romaine lettuce, coarsely chopped (6 cups)

1 cup grape or cherry tomatoes, halved

1. Preheat the oven to 400°F.
2. Sprinkle the chicken breasts with half of the garlic, ⅛ teaspoon of the salt, and the pepper. Sprinkle the zucchini with the remaining ⅛ teaspoon salt.
3. Spray a nonstick grill pan or skillet with nonstick spray and set over medium-high heat. Add the zucchini and cook until tender and browned, about 3 minutes on each side. Transfer the zucchini to a plate. Add the chicken breasts to the grill pan and cook until lightly browned and just cooked through, 4–5 minutes on each side.
4. Combine the remaining garlic and 2 tablespoons of the Parmesan cheese. Place the pitas rough-side up on a baking sheet and sprinkle with the cheese mixture. Bake until golden brown and crisp, 6–8 minutes.
5. Meanwhile, stack the zucchini slices and cut crosswise diagonally into 1-inch pieces. Thinly slice the chicken breasts on the diagonal.
6. Combine 1 tablespoon of the Parmesan cheese, the Caesar dressing, lemon juice, and mustard in a small bowl. Toss the zucchini, lettuce, and tomatoes with 2 tablespoons of the dressing mixture in a large bowl. Top the pitas evenly with the zucchini-salad mixture, then arrange the chicken on top. Drizzle each with the remaining dressing mixture, then sprinkle with the remaining Parmesan cheese.

Per serving (1 pizza): 284 Cal, 8 g Fat, 2 g Sat Fat, 67 mg Chol, 686 mg Sod, 22 g Carb, 3 g Fib, 32 g Prot, 160 mg Calc. *POINTS: 6.*

New Orleans
Sausage Pizza

New Orleans Sausage Pizza

Makes 4 servings

The base for this savory topping is what's known as the holy trinity of New Orleans cooking: onion, celery, and bell pepper. That, plus other New Orleans favorites—spicy andouille sausage and Cajun seasoning—make a pizza fit for any native of Louisianna. Use French bread that you can buy in the supermarket, one that isn't too dense or crusty, and not a baguette, which would be too narrow.

4 ounces andouille or other spicy smoked sausage, diced

1 small onion, chopped

1 small green bell pepper, seeded and chopped

1 small celery stalk, chopped

2 teaspoons homemade Cajun seasoning (see tip below)

1 cup Basic Tomato Sauce (page 12)

½ (8-ounce) loaf French bread

½ cup shredded smoked mozzarella cheese

1 scallion, thinly sliced

1. Preheat the oven to 425°F.
2. Spray a nonstick skillet with nonstick spray and set over medium-high heat. Add the sausage and cook, stirring, until browned, about 5 minutes. Remove the sausage and drain on paper towels. Wipe out any fat from the skillet.
3. Add the onion, bell pepper, and celery to the skillet. Cook over medium heat, stirring occasionally, until the vegetables are softened, about 8 minutes. Stir in the Cajun seasoning and cook 1 minute. Add the tomato sauce; bring to a simmer and cook 3 minutes.
4. Cut the bread in half horizontally and arrange, cut-side up, on a baking sheet. Spoon the vegetable sauce over the bread. Top with the sausage. Bake until heated through and the bread is browned at the edges, about 12 minutes. Sprinkle evenly with the cheese and scallion. Bake until the cheese melts, about 2 minutes. Cut each pizza in half, making a total of 4 pieces.

Per serving (1 piece): 322 Cal, 14 g Fat, 6 g Sat Fat, 27 mg Chol, 1069 mg Sod, 37 g Carb, 3 g Fib, 13 g Prot, 157 mg Calc. **POINTS: 7.**

 tip Some purchased Cajun seasoning blends are high in sodium. Here is our own low-salt blend: Combine 1 tablespoon paprika and 1 teaspoon each onion powder, garlic powder, salt, freshly ground pepper, dried thyme, dried oregano, and cayenne. It makes about 3 tablespoons and keeps well in a screw-top jar on the pantry shelf for up to one year.

Buffalo Chicken Pizzas

Makes 4 servings

Traditionally, buffalo wings are served with a hot sauce and accompanied by a blue-cheese dressing. Instead of the usual butter in the hot sauce to tame the heat, honey does the job here. Choose a mild brand of hot pepper sauce that has flavor, as well as heat, to help keep the fire at bay. To maintain the tradition of the blue-cheese accompaniment, serve these pizzas with a salad of iceberg lettuce, sliced celery, grated carrot, diced red onion, and for an extra *POINT*, 1 tablespoon of reduced-fat blue cheese dressing.

2 tablespoons hot pepper sauce
1 tablespoon Dijon mustard
1 tablespoon honey
½ pound skinless boneless chicken breasts, cut into bite-size pieces
2 Kaiser or hard rolls, halved horizontally
¼ cup canned tomato sauce
½ cup shredded Monterey Jack cheese

1. Preheat the oven to 425°F. Combine the hot pepper sauce, mustard, and honey in a small bowl. Toss the chicken and half of the hot pepper sauce mixture in a medium bowl; let marinate 15 minutes. Arrange the roll halves, cut-side up, on a baking sheet.

2. Spray a nonstick skillet with nonstick spray and set over medium-high heat. Cook the chicken, turning once, until browned and just cooked through, 3–4 minutes. Stir in the remaining hot pepper sauce mixture and the tomato sauce.

3. Spoon the chicken and sauce evenly onto the 4 roll halves, then sprinkle with the cheese. Bake until heated through and the cheese melts, 10–12 minutes.

Per serving (1 piece): 216 Cal, 7 g Fat, 3 g Sat Fat, 44 mg Chol, 439 mg Sod, 19 g Carb, 1 g Fib, 19 g Prot, 138 mg Calc. *POINTS: 5.*

 tip To save on cleanup, use scissors to cut the chicken breast into pieces and work over a paper plate. Shredded mozzarella cheese can be substituted for the Monterey Jack, if you like.

Tex-Mex Tostada Pizzas with Beef and Black Beans

Makes 4 servings

Beef for stir-fry can be used here. Just make sure that the strips are lean. And they should be thin enough—½ inch or less and about 3 inches long. Store-bought pizza sauce can be substituted for the homemade Roasted or Basic Tomato Sauce to save time.

4 (7-inch) fat-free flour tortillas

1 cup Basic Tomato Sauce (page 12) or Roasted Tomato Sauce (page 13)

½ (15½-ounce) can black beans, rinsed and drained

3 tablespoons chopped red onion

6 ounces lean beef round, trimmed of all visible fat and cut into thin strips

1 tablespoon taco seasoning

½ cup shredded pepperjack cheese

1 cup chopped iceberg lettuce

1 plum tomato, chopped

2 tablespoons chopped fresh cilantro

1 tablespoon reduced-fat bottled Italian dressing

1. Preheat the oven to 450°F. Place the tortillas on a large nonstick baking sheet. Spread ½ cup of the tomato sauce evenly on the tortillas to ½ inch from the edges. Sprinkle evenly with the beans and onion. Bake until browned at the edges, about 5 minutes.

2. Meanwhile, spray a nonstick skillet with nonstick spray and set over medium-high heat. Add the beef and stir-fry until browned but still rare inside, 1–2 minutes. Stir in the remaining ½ cup tomato sauce and the taco seasoning.

3. Spoon the beef mixture evenly onto the tortillas. Sprinkle with the cheese. Bake until the cheese melts, 1–2 minutes.

4. Toss the lettuce, tomato, cilantro, and dressing together in a medium bowl. Spoon on top of the pizzas just before serving.

Per serving (1 pizza): 282 Cal, 7 g Fat, 3 g Sat Fat, 36 mg Chol, 765 mg Sod, 36 g Carb, 5 g Fib, 19 g Prot, 199 mg Calc. ***POINTS: 5.***

Barbecued Chicken Pizzas

Makes 4 servings

Deli-roasted chicken helps keep these pizzas easy. Just be sure to remove the skin from the chicken before removing the meat from the bones and shredding it. Shredding the chicken by pulling it apart with your fingers is the fastest way of getting bite-size pieces.

4 whole-wheat English muffins, split

1 medium red onion, diced

1 red bell pepper, seeded and cut into bite-size pieces

½ cup bottled fat-free barbecue sauce

1½ cups shredded deli-roasted chicken

2 teaspoons hot pepper sauce

½ cup shredded light pizza cheese blend

1 tablespoon chopped fresh cilantro

1. Preheat the oven to 425°F. Place the English muffins, cut-side down, on a baking sheet. Bake until toasted, 6–8 minutes. Turn the muffins over and set aside.

2. Spray a large nonstick skillet with nonstick spray and set over medium heat. Add the onion and bell pepper; cook, stirring occasionally, until the onion is golden, about 12 minutes. Remove the skillet from the heat. Set aside 1 tablespoon barbecue sauce. Add the remaining barbecue sauce, the chicken, and the hot pepper sauce to the vegetables; stir until blended.

3. Spoon the chicken mixture onto the English muffins. Sprinkle evenly with the cheese. Bake until heated through and the cheese melts, 5–8 minutes. Drizzle with the reserved 1 tablespoon barbecue sauce, then sprinkle with the cilantro.

Per serving (2 pieces): 302 Cal, 7 g Fat, 3 g Sat Fat, 50 mg Chol, 895 mg Sod, 36 g Carb, 5 g Fib, 25 g Prot, 303 mg Calc. *POINTS: 6.*

 tip There is a vast array of packaged shredded cheeses in the supermarket, many of which are light or reduced-fat versions of the full-fat originals. Pizza cheese blend is a combination of shredded mozzarella and cheddar, and it comes in a light version. If you can't find this particular light cheese blend, try another.

The Right Stuff

Making top-quality pizza at home is easy with these handy tools.

Food Processor: While you can make dough by hand, the processor kneads dough in just about 1 minute.

Dough Scraper: A thin metal or plastic gadget that's great for lifting sticky dough or cutting it into pieces. It also scrapes up bits of dough from the work surface for easy cleanup.

Rolling Pin: Flattens dough evenly and eliminates air pockets. Especially good for making thin pizza crusts.

Pizza Pans: Look for dark metal pans instead of those made of stainless steel. Dark metal is a better conductor of heat and makes a crispier crust. Nonstick perforated pans are also a good choice.

Baking Sheets: If you don't have a pizza pan, use a baking sheet with no rim on at least one side. This makes sliding the pizza off the pan easy.

Nonstick Pans: If using nonstick pizza pans or baking sheets, there is no need to spray with nonstick spray. Simply place the dough directly on the pan.

Baking or Pizza Stone: An essential item for brick oven–style pizza. Ceramic holds heat well, keeping the temperature steady. And because it's porous, moisture is pulled from the dough, producing a crustier pizza. It is important to preheat the stone in the oven for at least 20 minutes before using.

Pizza Peel: A large wooden paddle used to place pizza on a heated baking stone and to remove it from the oven.

Pizza Cutter: This sturdy metal wheel makes slicing even deep-dish pizza a breeze.

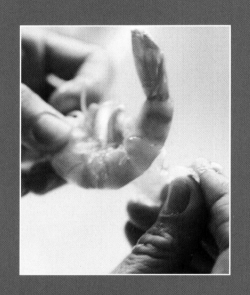

Coastal Combos

Shrimp, Scallops, and More Favorite Toppings

Tuna Niçoise on Potato-Rosemary Pizza

Makes 8 servings

Although there are a few steps to this recipe, it's simple to prepare, and the results are terrific. Just be sure to have all your ingredients ready to go before you begin.

1 baking potato, peeled and cut into ⅛-inch slices

½ recipe (about 1 pound) Basic Pizza Dough (page 10), at room temperature

3 tablespoons chopped fresh rosemary

2 (6-ounce) tuna steaks

½ teaspoon salt

½ teaspoon ground pepper

2 teaspoons olive oil

3 tablespoons white balsamic vinegar

1 teaspoon fresh lemon juice

1 teaspoon Dijon mustard

2 tomatoes, cut into thin wedges

1 small red onion, halved lengthwise, then thinly sliced crosswise

8 niçoise olives, pitted and chopped

1 tablespoon capers, drained

¼ cup thinly sliced fresh basil

1. Cook the potato in enough boiling water to cover, in a small saucepan, until tender, about 8 minutes; drain.

2. Arrange one rack on the bottom rung of the oven. Preheat the oven to 450°F. Spray a 10½ × 15½ -inch jelly-roll pan with olive-oil nonstick spray.

3. Sprinkle a work surface lightly with flour. Turn the dough onto the surface; knead lightly. With lightly floured hands, stretch and press the dough onto the bottom of the pan.

4. Arrange the potato slices on the dough. Sprinkle with the rosemary, then lightly spray with olive-oil nonstick spray. Bake on the bottom rack of the oven until the crust is golden on the bottom, about 20 minutes.

5. Meanwhile, sprinkle the tuna with ¼ teaspoon of the salt and ¼ teaspoon of the pepper. Heat a medium non-stick skillet over high heat. Swirl in 1 teaspoon of the oil, then add the tuna. Cook until browned on the outside and pink in the center, about 3 minutes on each side for medium-rare. Remove from the heat and let rest 5 minutes, then cut into 1½-inch chunks.

6. To prepare the dressing, whisk together the vinegar, lemon juice, mustard, remaining 1 teaspoon oil, remaining ¼ teaspoon salt, and remaining ¼ teaspoon pepper.

7. Top the pizza with the tuna, tomatoes, onion, olives, and capers. Sprinkle with the dressing and basil.

Per serving (⅛ of pizza): 237 Cal, 6 g Fat, 1 g Sat Fat, 16 mg Chol, 449 mg Sod, 32 g Carb, 2 g Fib, 14 g Prot, 24 mg Calc. **POINTS: 5.**

 tip White balsamic vinegar has a sweet, mellow flavor, making it a perfect partner for fresh tuna. It is available in most supermarkets.

Lobster, Goat Cheese, and Sun-Dried Tomato Pizza

Makes 6 servings

Truly a gourmet pizza, this is equally delicious with cooked crabmeat or shrimp. If you're on a budget, try surimi (imitation crabmeat). The yellow bell peppers are broiled, adding a wonderfully smoky flavor to the pizza. Substitute red or orange bell peppers if you like. Or if time is short, use jarred roasted red bell peppers.

3 yellow bell peppers

8 cups water

2 (4-ounce) frozen rock lobster tails

½ recipe (about 1 pound) Basic Pizza Dough (page 10), at room temperature

1 small red onion, cut into thin rings

¼ cup oil-packed sun-dried tomatoes, drained, patted dry, and cut into thin slices

4 ounces reduced-fat goat cheese, crumbled

½ cup torn fresh basil leaves

1. Preheat the broiler. Line a baking sheet with foil; place the bell peppers on the baking sheet. Broil 5 inches from the heat, turning frequently with tongs, until lightly charred, about 10 minutes. Wrap the bell peppers in the foil and let steam for 10 minutes. When cool enough to handle, peel, discard the seeds, and cut into ¼-inch strips.

2. Meanwhile, bring the water to a boil in a saucepan. Add the lobster tails and cook until they are bright red, 8–10 minutes. Rinse under cold running water to cool; drain. When the lobster tails are cool enough to handle, gently pull the meat from the shells and cut into 1-inch chunks.

3. Arrange one rack on the bottom rung of the oven. Preheat the oven to 500°F.

4. Sprinkle a work surface lightly with flour. Turn the dough onto the surface; knead lightly. With a lightly floured rolling pin, roll into a 12-inch circle. Transfer the circle of dough to a nonstick pizza pan or large baking sheet, gently pulling the dough back to a 12-inch circle.

5. Scatter the roasted peppers, onion, and sun-dried tomatoes on the dough; sprinkle with the cheese. Bake on the bottom rack of the oven until the crust is golden and the cheese melts slightly, about 15 minutes. Top with the lobster and continue to bake until the lobster is just heated through, about 3 minutes. Sprinkle with the basil just before serving.

Per serving (⅙ of pizza): 236 Cal, 4 g Fat, 2 g Sat Fat, 23 mg Chol, 403 mg Sod, 40 g Carb, 3 g Fib, 10 g Prot, 120 mg Calc. **POINTS: 4.**

Shrimp Creole Pizza

Makes 6 servings

Traditionally, shrimp Creole is served on a bed of hot cooked rice, but a crispy pizza crust makes a truly special base for this favorite dish. If you like, make the sauce, without adding the shrimp, the day before. The flavors will blend and mellow overnight. For the landlubber, substitute strips of cooked chicken or turkey for the shrimp.

½ recipe (about 1 pound) Basic Pizza Dough (page 10), at room temperature
2 teaspoons canola oil
1 onion, thinly sliced
1 green bell pepper, seeded and thinly sliced
2 garlic cloves, minced
1 (14½-ounce) can stewed tomatoes
½ cup water
1 tablespoon Cajun seasoning
½ pound large shrimp, peeled and deveined
1 cup shredded part-skim mozzarella cheese
2 tablespoons chopped fresh parsley

1. Arrange one rack on the bottom rung of the oven. Preheat the oven to 450°F. Spray a pizza pan or large baking sheet with olive-oil nonstick spray.

2. Sprinkle a work surface lightly with flour. Turn the dough onto the surface; knead lightly. With a lightly floured rolling pin, roll into a 12-inch circle. Transfer the circle of dough to the pizza pan or baking sheet, gently pulling the dough back to a 12-inch circle. Bake on the bottom rack of the oven until the crust is lightly browned, 15–20 minutes.

3. Meanwhile, heat the oil in a large nonstick skillet over medium-high heat. Add the onion, bell pepper, and garlic. Cook, stirring frequently, until the vegetables are tender, about 8 minutes. Add the tomatoes, water, and Cajun seasoning; bring to a boil. Reduce the heat and simmer, uncovered, until the sauce is slightly thickened, about 10 minutes. Remove from the heat and stir in the shrimp.

4. Spread the shrimp mixture over the dough, then sprinkle with the cheese. Bake on the bottom rack of the oven until the crust is golden and the shrimp is just opaque in the center, 4–5 minutes. Sprinkle with the parsley just before serving.

Per serving (⅙ of pizza): 292 Cal, 7 g Fat, 3 g Sat Fat, 46 mg Chol, 894 mg Sod, 43 g Carb, 3 g Fib, 15 g Prot, 178 mg Calc. **POINTS: 6.**

 **CUT POINTS** Use fat-free mozzarella instead of part-skim and substitute a spritz of nonstick spray for the 2 teaspoons oil to sauté the vegetables. You'll save a **POINT** per serving.

Deep-Dish Scallop and Spinach Pizza

Makes 6 servings

Like all seafood, scallops perish quickly, so use them within one to two days of buying. Look for scallops with a sweet, fresh smell and a moist sheen. To avoid excess moisture on your pizza, be sure to pat the scallops dry with paper towels before using.

½ recipe (about 1 pound) Basic Pizza Dough (page 10), at room temperature

2 teaspoons olive oil

1 onion, thinly sliced

2 garlic cloves, chopped

1 (10-ounce) package frozen chopped spinach, thawed and squeezed dry

¼ teaspoon salt

¾ cup part-skim ricotta cheese

½ pound sea scallops, patted dry and cut horizontally in half

3 ounces reduced-fat feta cheese, crumbled

1. Arrange one rack on the bottom rung of the oven. Preheat the oven to 450°F. Spray a 12-inch cast-iron skillet or deep-dish pizza pan with nonstick spray.

2. Sprinkle a work surface lightly with flour. Turn the dough onto the surface; knead lightly. With a lightly floured rolling pin, roll into a 13-inch circle. Transfer the circle of dough to the skillet, gently pulling the dough halfway up the sides of the skillet. Spray the top of the dough with olive-oil nonstick spray. Bake on the bottom rack of the oven until the dough begins to puff up slightly and the bottom just begins to brown (use a narrow metal spatula to lift the bottom of the dough to check for browning), about 20 minutes.

3. Meanwhile, heat a large nonstick skillet over medium heat. Swirl in the oil, then add the onion and garlic. Cook, stirring occasionally, until the onion is golden, about 8 minutes. Stir in the spinach and salt. Cook until the spinach begins to soften, about 3 minutes. Remove from the heat and set aside.

4. Spread the ricotta cheese evenly over the pizza crust. Top with the spinach mixture, the scallops, then the feta cheese. Bake until heated through and the scallops are just opaque in the center, 6–8 minutes.

Per serving (⅙ of pizza): 300 Cal, 7 g Fat, 2 g Sat Fat, 30 mg Chol, 677 mg Sod, 41 g Carb, 3 g Fib, 17 g Prot, 240 mg Calc. *POINTS: 6.*

 tip If you use a skillet without an ovenproof handle to make this pizza, be sure to cover the handle with heavy-duty foil to protect it from the heat.

**Deep-Dish Mussels
Fra Diavolo Pizza**

Deep-Dish Mussels Fra Diavolo Pizza

Makes 6 servings

This pizza and the previous one are baked in large cast-iron skillets. If you don't have one, use a deep-dish pizza pan or large regular skillet instead. If the handle on your regular skillet is not ovenproof, be sure to cover it with heavy-duty foil.

1 cup reduced-sodium chicken broth

1 dozen mussels, scrubbed and debearded

1½ cups Basic Tomato Sauce (page 12) or Roasted Tomato Sauce (page 13)

¼ teaspoon crushed red pepper

½ recipe (about 1 pound) Basic Pizza Dough (page 10), at room temperature

¾ cup shredded part-skim mozzarella cheese

2 tablespoons thinly sliced fresh basil

1 tablespoon grated Parmesan cheese

1. Arrange one rack on the bottom rung of the oven. Preheat the oven to 500°F. Spray a 12-inch cast-iron skillet or deep-dish pizza pan with nonstick spray.

2. Discard any mussels that are slightly open and do not close when gently tapped. Bring the broth to a boil in a medium saucepan. Add the mussels. Cover and cook, shaking the pan, until the mussels open, 5–7 minutes. Remove the mussels from their shells (discard any mussels that do not open). Transfer the mussels to a bowl. Stir in the tomato sauce and crushed red pepper; set aside.

3. Sprinkle a work surface lightly with flour. Turn the dough onto the surface; knead lightly. With a lightly floured rolling pin, roll into a 13-inch circle. Transfer the circle of dough to the skillet, gently pulling and stretching the dough halfway up the sides of the skillet. Spray the top of the dough with olive-oil nonstick spray. Bake on the bottom rack of the oven until the dough begins to puff slightly and the bottom just begins to brown (use a narrow metal spatula to lift the bottom of the dough to check for browning), about 20 minutes.

4. Spoon the mussel mixture onto the dough, then top with the mozzarella cheese. Bake until the crust is golden and the cheese melts, about 10 minutes. Sprinkle with the basil and Parmesan cheese just before serving.

Per serving (⅙ of pizza): 268 Cal, 5 g Fat, 2 g Sat Fat, 19 mg Chol, 928 mg Sod, 40 g Carb, 2 g Fib, 15 g Prot, 152 mg Calc. *POINTS: 5.*

 tip Mussels sold in many markets today are farm-raised, so they're free of the small hair-like cords known as beards. If your mussels have beards, simply grab them between your fingers and twist to remove.

Anchovy, Onion, and Olive Pizza

Makes 6 servings

All the flavors in this pizza are typical of the classic French pizza, *pissaladière*. If they're available, use Vidalia onions for a sweet, mellow flavor.

2 teaspoons olive oil

2 Vidalia onions or 3 yellow onions, halved lengthwise, then thinly sliced crosswise

2 garlic cloves, chopped

¼ cup dry white wine

½ teaspoon sugar

¼ teaspoon salt

12 kalamata olives, pitted and chopped

4 flat anchovies, rinsed, patted dry, and coarsely chopped

1 tablespoon chopped fresh thyme, or 1 teaspoon dried

½ recipe (about 1 pound) Basic Pizza Dough (page 10), at room temperature

1. Heat a large nonstick skillet over medium-high heat. Swirl in the oil, then add the onions, garlic, wine, sugar, and salt; bring to a boil. Reduce the heat and simmer, covered, until the onions are well softened, about 20 minutes. Remove from the heat then stir in the olives, anchovies, and thyme; set aside.

2. Arrange one rack on the bottom rung of the oven. Preheat the oven to 500°F.

3. Sprinkle a work surface lightly with flour. Turn the dough onto the surface; knead lightly. With a lightly floured rolling pin, roll into a 12-inch circle. Transfer the circle of dough to a nonstick pizza pan or large baking sheet, gently pulling the dough back to a 12-inch circle.

4. Spread the onion mixture over the dough. Bake on the bottom rack of the oven until the crust is golden, 12–15 minutes.

Per serving (⅙ of pizza): 240 Cal, 4 g Fat, 1 g Sat Fat, 2 mg Chol, 560 mg Sod, 43 g Carb, 3 g Fib, 7 g Prot, 42 mg Calc. **POINTS: 5.**

 For a party appetizer, bake the pizza in a jelly-roll pan (about 10 × 15 inches) and cut into 12 squares.

Tuna, Olive, and Roasted Pepper Pizza

Makes 8 servings

A seasoned, creamy-white bean puree serves as a wonderfully flavorful base (with little fat) for this easy pizza. Canned tuna, jarred roasted red peppers, and precrumbled feta cheese also keep with the "easy" theme. You can use canned salmon in place of the tuna if you like.

1 (14-ounce) can cannellini (white kidney) beans, rinsed and drained

1 tablespoon fresh lemon juice

2 teaspoons extra-virgin olive oil

1 garlic clove, chopped

1 (10-ounce) thin prebaked pizza crust

2 (6-ounce) cans solid white tuna packed in water, drained

½ cup roasted red pepper strips

10 kalamata olives, pitted and chopped

⅓ cup reduced-fat feta cheese, crumbled

3 tablespoons coarsely chopped fresh oregano

1. Preheat the oven to 450°F.
2. Puree the beans, lemon juice, oil, and garlic in a food processor. Spread the bean mixture evenly onto the pizza crust. Top with the tuna, red peppers, olives, and cheese.
3. Place the pizza crust on a nonstick pizza pan or baking sheet. Bake until heated through and the cheese melts slightly, 8–10 minutes. Sprinkle with the oregano just before serving.

Per serving (⅛ of pizza): 221 Cal, 5 g Fat, 1 g Sat Fat, 17 mg Chol, 511 mg Sod, 28 g Carb, 4 g Fib, 16 g Prot, 66 mg Calc. *POINTS: 4.*

 tip For a delicious pizza wrap, spread the bean puree on 4 burrito-size, fat-free flour tortillas. Top with the remaining ingredients, then roll up. Cut in half and serve cold.

White Clam Pizza

Makes 6 servings

The trick to keeping the seafood on a seafood pizza from overcooking in the oven is to either prebake a homemade crust yourself or use a store-bought prebaked crust. The store-bought prebaked crust heats through in about the same amount of time it takes to reheat the seafood.

2 teaspoons extra-virgin olive oil

2 shallots, thinly sliced

4 garlic cloves, thinly sliced

1 tomato, chopped

¼ teaspoon salt

¼ cup dry white wine

¼ cup bottled clam juice

3 (6½-ounce) cans chopped clams, liquid drained and reserved

¼ cup chopped fresh parsley

1 (10-ounce) thin prebaked pizza crust

⅔ cup shredded part-skim mozzarella cheese

1. Arrange one rack on the bottom rung of the oven. Preheat the oven to 475°F.

2. Heat a medium nonstick skillet over medium-high heat. Swirl in the oil, then add the shallots and garlic. Cook, stirring occasionally, until golden, 2–3 minutes. Add the tomato and salt. Cook, stirring, until softened, about 2 minutes. Stir in the wine, the clam juice, and the reserved clam liquid; bring to a boil. Cook until the flavors are blended and the liquid reduces slightly, about 3 minutes. Remove from the heat, then stir in the clams and parsley.

3. Place the pizza crust on a nonstick pizza pan or baking sheet. Spoon the clam mixture onto the crust. Sprinkle with the cheese. Bake on the bottom rack of the oven until the pizza is heated through and the cheese melts, about 8 minutes.

Per serving (⅙ of pizza): 255 Cal, 7 g Fat, 2 g Sat Fat, 35 mg Chol, 456 mg Sod, 28 g Carb, 2 g Fib, 18 g Prot, 152 mg Calc. *POINTS: 5.*

Seafood Pizza with Artichokes

Makes 8 servings

Surimi is a delicate, sweet-tasting blend of seafoods often used in California rolls. Also sold as "imitation crabmeat," it's a tasty, economical, substitute for higher-priced crabmeat and lobster.

1 tablespoon olive oil

2 tablespoons all-purpose flour

1 cup fat-free milk

1 (14-ounce) can artichoke hearts packed in water, drained, patted dry, and cut in half

8 ounces surimi

1 (16-ounce) thick prebaked pizza crust

⅔ cup shredded light Havarti cheese

1 tablespoon grated Parmesan cheese

1. Preheat the oven to 450°F.

2. Heat a medium nonstick saucepan over medium heat. Swirl in the oil, then stir in the flour. Cook, stirring constantly, until the flour turns golden, about 2 minutes. Whisk in the milk and cook, stirring constantly, until the sauce boils and thickens slightly, about 6 minutes. Remove from the heat, then stir in the artichoke hearts and surimi.

3. Place the pizza crust on a pizza pan or baking sheet. Spoon the artichoke mixture on top. Sprinkle with the Havarti cheese, then the Parmesan cheese. Bake until heated through and the cheese melts, about 10 minutes.

Per serving (⅛ of pizza): 270 Cal, 6 g Fat, 2 g Sat Fat, 15 mg Chol, 678 mg Sod, 39 g Carb, 3 g Fib, 14 g Prot, 144 mg Calc. *POINTS: 5.*

 CUT POINTS Substitute a (10-ounce) thin prebaked pizza crust for the thick crust and save almost *2 POINTS* per serving.

Seared-Salmon Pizzas with Arugula and Shaved Parmesan

Seared-Salmon Pizzas with Arugula and Shaved Parmesan

Makes 4 servings

The flavors of salmon, fresh dill, horseradish, arugula, and Parmesan cheese marry well in this simple and delicious no-bake pizza. Be sure to wash the arugula thoroughly, as it can be quite sandy. To save time, look for prewashed arugula sold in 4-ounce bags. If you can't find arugula, watercress makes an excellent substitute.

6 ounces fat-free cream cheese

¼ cup chopped fresh dill

1 tablespoon grated lemon zest

1 tablespoon fresh lemon juice

1 teaspoon prepared horseradish

4 drops hot pepper sauce

1 bunch arugula, cleaned and coarsely chopped

2 tablespoons white balsamic vinegar

½ teaspoon salt

2 (6-ounce) salmon fillets

1 teaspoon canola oil

2 (9-inch) whole-wheat lavash breads or tortillas

½ small red onion, cut crosswise into thin slices

2-ounce piece Parmesan cheese, shaved

½ teaspoon freshly ground pepper

1. Combine the cream cheese, 2 tablespoons of the dill, the lemon zest, lemon juice, horseradish, and hot pepper sauce in a small bowl. Cover and refrigerate until ready to use. Toss the arugula with the vinegar and ¼ teaspoon of the salt in a medium bowl; set aside.

2. Rub the salmon fillets with the remaining 2 tablespoons dill and the remaining ¼ teaspoon salt. Heat a medium nonstick skillet over medium-high heat. Swirl in the oil, then add the salmon. Cook until browned on the outside and just opaque in the center, about 4 minutes on each side. Remove from the heat and let rest 5 minutes, then cut into 1½-inch chunks.

3. Meanwhile, spray a large nonstick skillet with nonstick spray and set over medium-high heat. Add one lavash and cook, turning occasionally, until crisp and golden, about 4 minutes. Repeat with the remaining lavash. Remove from the heat and let cool slightly.

4. Spread the cream cheese mixture onto each lavash. Top each evenly with the arugula mixture, salmon, onion, Parmesan cheese, and pepper. Cut each pizza in half.

Per serving (½ of one pizza): 290 Cal, 11 g Fat, 4 g Sat Fat, 68 mg Chol, 917 mg Sod, 14 g Carb, 2 g Fib, 33 g Prot, 306 mg Calc. **_POINTS: 6._**

Pesto-Scallop and Arugula Pizza

Makes 6 servings

Pine nuts sprinkled over pesto-tossed scallops, along with peppery arugula, make this a different yet delicious pizza—and one that can be put together in under 20 minutes. Ready-to-bake pizza crusts are partially baked and come in a variety of sizes. Here we use one (12-inch) crust, from a two-crust (16-ounce) package, found in the refrigerator section of the supermarket. Use a 10-ounce prebaked thin pizza crust if you prefer.

½ pound sea scallops, patted dry and cut horizontally in half

1 tablespoon prepared pesto

1 (12-inch) ready-to-bake pizza crust

⅔ cup Basic Tomato Sauce (page 12) or Roasted Tomato Sauce (page 13)

1 cup arugula leaves

1 tablespoon pine nuts

1-ounce piece Parmesan cheese, shaved

1. Arrange one rack on the bottom rung of the oven. Preheat the oven to 450°F.

2. Combine the scallops and pesto in a medium bowl; toss to coat and set aside.

3. Place the pizza crust on a nonstick pizza pan or baking sheet. Spoon the tomato sauce evenly onto the crust. Top with the arugula, then the scallop mixture. Sprinkle with the pine nuts.

4. Bake on the bottom rack of the oven until the crust is golden and crisp and the scallops are opaque in the center, 8–10 minutes. Sprinkle with the Parmesan cheese just before serving.

Per serving (⅙ of pizza): 199 Cal, 7 g Fat, 2 g Sat Fat, 12 mg Chol, 524 mg Sod, 24 g Carb, 1 g Fib, 11 g Prot, 117 mg Calc. **POINTS: 4.**

 tip To shave Parmesan cheese, run a vegetable peeler along the length of a block of Parmesan cheese. Keep the shavings refrigerated if you're not using them right away.

Italian Bread Pizza with Sardines

Makes 6 servings 🕐

Canned sardines—like canned salmon—are a good source of calcium, as well as protein, vitamins, and other minerals. The calcium comes from the bones, which are softened during the canning process, making them perfectly edible. Italian bread, a nice alternative to traditional pizza crust, makes this a cinch to put together.

1 (8-ounce) loaf Italian bread

1 tablespoon extra-virgin olive oil

1 tablespoon chopped fresh parsley

1 garlic clove, chopped

½ teaspoon dried oregano

¼ teaspoon crushed red pepper

2 (3¾-ounce) cans water-packed sardines, drained

½ cup shredded part-skim mozzarella cheese

1. Preheat the broiler.
2. Slice the bread horizontally, then cut each half crosswise in thirds, making a total of 6 pieces.
3. Combine the oil, parsley, garlic, oregano, and crushed red pepper in a small bowl. Brush each piece of bread with the oil mixture. Place on a broiler rack and broil 6 inches from the heat until the bread is lightly browned, about 5 minutes.
4. Arrange the sardines on the bread pieces, then sprinkle evenly with the cheese. Broil 6 inches from the heat until heated through and the cheese melts, about 3 minutes.

Per serving (1 piece): 199 Cal, 8 g Fat, 2 g Sat Fat, 24 mg Chol, 299 mg Sod, 19 g Carb, 1 g Fib, 11 g Prot, 119 mg Calc. **POINTS: 4.**

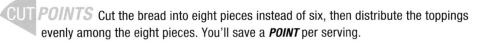 **CUT POINTS** Cut the bread into eight pieces instead of six, then distribute the toppings evenly among the eight pieces. You'll save a **POINT** per serving.

Southwestern Shrimp-and-Sausage Pizzas

Makes 4 servings

Italian turkey sausage, available hot or sweet, is an excellent, well-flavored alternative to high-fat pork sausage. We find the sweet sausage paired with mild salsa and a few chopped green chiles gives a heat level suited to most people, but use the hot sausage and spicy salsa if you like fiery flavors.

2 teaspoons olive oil

1 onion, thinly sliced

½ pound sweet Italian turkey sausage, casings removed and crumbled

2 garlic cloves, chopped

½ pound small shrimp, peeled and deveined

1 cup prepared mild salsa

2 tablespoons canned chopped green chiles

½ teaspoon ground cumin

4 (6-inch) corn tortillas

½ cup shredded reduced-fat cheddar cheese

1. Arrange one rack on the bottom rung of the oven. Preheat the oven to 500°F.

2. Heat a large nonstick skillet over medium-high heat. Swirl in the oil, then add the onion. Cook, stirring frequently, until softened, about 4 minutes. Add the sausage and garlic. Cook, stirring occasionally, until the sausage is browned, 6–8 minutes. Add the shrimp, salsa, chiles, and cumin; bring to a boil. Reduce the heat and simmer, uncovered, until the shrimp just begin to turn pink, about 5 minutes. Remove from the heat.

3. Spray a medium nonstick skillet with nonstick spray and set over medium-high heat. Add one tortilla and cook, turning occasionally, until crisp and golden, about 5 minutes. Repeat with the remaining tortillas.

4. Arrange the tortillas on a nonstick baking sheet. Spoon the sausage-and-shrimp mixture onto the tortillas. Sprinkle evenly with the cheese. Bake on the bottom rack of the oven until heated through and the cheese melts, about 5 minutes.

Per serving (1 pizza): 244 Cal, 10 g Fat, 3 g Sat Fat, 88 mg Chol, 761 mg Sod, 19 g Carb, 3 g Fib, 20 g Prot, 206 mg Calc. **POINTS: 5.**

 tip If you own a pizza stone, preheat the stone in the oven for at least 30 minutes. Omit Step 3 and place the tortillas on the stone instead of the baking sheet. Add the toppings and bake on the bottom rack of the oven, about 5 minutes.

Southwestern Shrimp-
and-Sausage Pizzas

Mini Mexi-Pizzas with Sole

Makes 4 servings

Because of their coarse texture, cornflake crumbs add crunch as well as flavor to any food. These sole fillets are no exception. Corn and green bell pepper add even more satisfying bite, flavor, and color.

1 teaspoon olive oil
1 onion, finely chopped
1 green bell pepper, seeded and chopped
¼ teaspoon salt
1 cup Basic Tomato Sauce (page 12) or Roasted Tomato Sauce (page 13)
½ cup fresh or thawed frozen corn kernels
4 (6-inch) corn tortillas
1 tablespoon low-fat mayonnaise
1 teaspoon low-fat (1%) milk
4 (4-ounce) sole or flounder fillets
½ cup cornflake crumbs
½ cup shredded reduced-fat Monterey Jack cheese
2 tablespoons sliced pitted ripe olives

1. Heat a large nonstick skillet over medium-high heat. Swirl in the oil, then add the onion, bell pepper, and salt. Cook, stirring occasionally, until softened, about 8 minutes. Stir in the tomato sauce and corn; cook until heated through. Remove from the heat and set aside.

2. Spray a medium nonstick skillet with nonstick spray and set over medium-high heat. Add one tortilla and cook, turning occasionally, until crisp and golden, about 5 minutes. Repeat with the remaining tortillas.

3. Preheat the oven to 425°F. Spray a nonstick baking sheet with nonstick spray.

4. Combine the mayonnaise and milk in a medium bowl. Add the sole fillets and toss to coat. Place the cornflake crumbs in a large zip-close plastic bag. Add the fillets and shake until coated. Place the fillets on the baking sheet. Bake, without turning, until the fillets are cooked through and browned, about 6 minutes.

5. Place the tortillas on another nonstick baking sheet. Arrange the fish fillets on the tortillas. Spoon the sauce over the fillets, then sprinkle evenly with the cheese and olives. Bake until heated through and the cheese melts, about 7 minutes.

Per serving (1 pizza): 280 Cal, 6 g Fat, 2 g Sat Fat, 61 mg Chol, 846 mg Sod, 30 g Carb, 4 g Fib, 27 g Prot, 184 mg Calc. *POINTS: 5.*

Tuna-Tomato Pizza Melts

Makes 4 servings

Tuna melts take on a slightly different twist with Mediterranean flavors of tomatoes, olives, and capers—a nice change from standard tuna salad. If the kids object, leave out the olives and capers and top their muffins with a little extra shredded cheese.

2 (6-ounce) cans solid white tuna packed in water, drained
6 tablespoons fat-free mayonnaise
¼ cup finely chopped red onion
10 kalamata olives, pitted and chopped
1 tablespoon small capers, drained
1 tablespoon chopped fresh parsley
2 sandwich-size English muffins, split and toasted
1 small tomato, chopped
½ cup shredded light Jarlsberg cheese

1. Preheat the broiler. Combine the tuna, mayonnaise, onion, olives, capers, and parsley in a medium bowl.
2. Spread the tuna mixture onto the muffin halves. Top evenly with the tomato and cheese. Arrange on a baking sheet and broil 3–4 inches from the heat until heated through and the cheese melts, about 3 minutes.

Per serving (1 pizza): 230 Cal, 5 g Fat, 2 g Sat Fat, 30 mg Chol, 766 mg Sod, 20 g Carb, 2 g Fib, 26 g Prot, 171 mg Calc. *POINTS: 5.*

 tip To save cleanup time, line the baking sheet with foil. English muffins now come in a convenient, large sandwich size (about 4 inches) and can be found in most supermarkets.

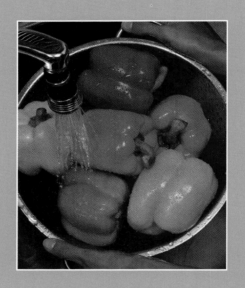

Veggie Slices

No-Meat Pizzas

Traditional Cheese Pizza

Makes 6 servings

If you have a yen for a plain ol' slice o' pizza, but don't want to spend all your *POINTS,* our version is the way to go. If time is short, substitute a 1-pound package of fresh pizza dough from the refrigerator section at the supermarket, for the homemade dough. If you don't have a pizza pan, use a baking sheet with no rim on at least one side, so you can easily slide the pizza off the pan onto a board for cutting.

½ recipe (about 1 pound) Basic Pizza Dough (page 10), at room temperature

2 cups Basic Tomato Sauce (page 12) or Roasted Tomato Sauce (page 13)

¾ cup shredded part-skim mozzarella cheese

2 tablespoons grated Parmesan or pecorino Romano cheese

2 tablespoons chopped fresh oregano or basil

1. Arrange one rack on the bottom rung of the oven. Preheat the oven to 500°F.
2. Sprinkle a work surface lightly with flour. Turn the dough onto the surface; knead lightly. With a lightly floured rolling pin, roll into a 12-inch circle. Transfer the circle of dough to a nonstick pizza pan or baking sheet, gently pulling the dough back to a 12-inch circle.
3. Spread the tomato sauce over the dough, then sprinkle with the mozzarella and Parmesan cheeses. Bake on the bottom rack of the oven until the crust is golden and the cheeses melt, 12–15 minutes. Sprinkle with the oregano just before serving.

Per serving (⅙ of pizza): 257 Cal, 6 g Fat, 2 g Sat Fat, 9 mg Chol, 478 mg Sod, 41 g Carb, 3 g Fib, 11 g Prot, 155 mg Calc. *POINTS: 5.*

 Parmesan and Romano cheeses—both full-flavored hard Italian cheeses—are often used interchangeably. Italy's preeminent Parmesan cheese, Parmigiano-Reggiano, is incomparable, with its complex, sharp flavor and granular texture, while Romano cheese—in particular, pecorino Romano—is enjoyed for its sharp, tangy flavor.

Piquillo Pepper Pizzettes

Makes 4 servings

Need a fast but healthy lunch? Here's your answer—an artichoke-and-sweet pepper English muffin pizza with peppery goat cheese. We use red piquillo sweet peppers from northern Spain that are slow-roasted over wood fires, giving them a rich, spicy-sweet flavor. The four-pepper goat cheese—containing black, green, pink, and white peppers—adds kick. Use regular goat cheese if you want a more subtle flavor.

1 (4-ounce) package four-pepper goat cheese

4 whole-wheat English muffins, split and toasted

4 scallions, thinly sliced (whites and 2 inches of green portion only)

4 canned artichoke hearts, drained and halved

1 cup sliced roasted red piquillo sweet peppers

1. Preheat the broiler. Spread half of the cheese on the toasted English muffin halves. Sprinkle a few scallion slices over each. Top each with an artichoke heart half, then the sweet peppers. Sprinkle the remaining cheese over all.

2. Place the muffins on a baking sheet and broil 5 inches from the heat until heated through and the cheese melts slightly, 2–3 minutes.

Per serving (2 pieces): 264 Cal, 10 g Fat, 6 g Sat Fat, 22 mg Chol, 742 mg Sod, 35 g Carb, 5 g Fib, 12 g Prot, 264 mg Calc. **POINTS: 5.**

tip Canned artichoke hearts can be waterlogged, so gently squeeze out the water before using. Look for red piquillo sweet peppers in cans in large supermarkets and some specialty stores. If you can't find them, substitute roasted red bell peppers or pimientos.

Pissaladière Squares with Tomato Coulis and Goat Cheese

Pissaladière Squares with Tomato Coulis and Goat Cheese

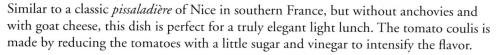

Makes 6 servings

Similar to a classic *pissaladière* of Nice in southern France, but without anchovies and with goat cheese, this dish is perfect for a truly elegant light lunch. The tomato coulis is made by reducing the tomatoes with a little sugar and vinegar to intensify the flavor.

1 teaspoon olive oil

1 Vidalia onion or 2 yellow onions, halved lengthwise, then thinly sliced crosswise

¼ teaspoon salt

2 teaspoons butter

8 small tomatoes, chopped (about 3½ cups)

1 teaspoon sugar

1 tablespoon balsamic vinegar

½ recipe (about 1 pound) Basic Pizza Dough (page 10), at room temperature

4 ounces goat cheese, crumbled

10 niçoise or other small oil-cured black olives, pitted and chopped

1 tablespoon chopped fresh thyme, or 1 teaspoon dried

1. Heat a large nonstick skillet over medium heat. Swirl in the oil, then add the onion and salt. Cook, stirring frequently, until the onion is golden, about 15 minutes. Transfer the onion to a plate and set aside.

2. To make the tomato coulis, melt the butter in the same skillet; add the tomatoes and sugar. Cook, stirring frequently, until most of the liquid has evaporated, about 10 minutes. Add the vinegar and simmer, about 1 minute.

3. Arrange one rack on the bottom rung of the oven. Preheat the oven to 450°F.

4. With floured hands, stretch and press the pizza dough onto the bottom of a 10½ × 15½-inch nonstick jelly-roll pan. Spread the onion onto the dough. Spoon the tomato coulis on top. Sprinkle evenly with the goat cheese, olives, and thyme.

5. Bake on the bottom rack of the oven until the crust is golden and the cheese is slightly melted, 15–20 minutes. Cut into 6 squares.

Per serving (1 square): 313 Cal, 11 g Fat, 5 g Sat Fat, 18 mg Chol, 587 mg Sod, 42 g Carb, 3 g Fib, 10 g Prot, 77 mg Calc. **POINTS: 7.**

tip The thinner the pizza crust, the fewer the toppings it will hold, so don't be tempted to load on extra ingredients.

Pizza Margherita with Roasted Grape Tomatoes

Makes 4 servings

Sweet, intense flavor from roasted grape tomatoes, a touch of Parmesan, and fresh basil are the simple yet classic toppings that make this pizza exceptional. Keeping the salt to a minimum allows the fresh flavor of the tomatoes to shine.

2 pints grape tomatoes, cut in half

1 large red onion, halved lengthwise, then sliced crosswise

2 large garlic cloves, sliced

1 tablespoon balsamic vinegar

¼ teaspoon salt

¼ teaspoon freshly ground pepper

½ recipe (about 1 pound) Basic Pizza Dough— semolina variation (page 11), at room temperature

1 (1-ounce) piece Parmesan cheese, shaved

12 fresh basil leaves, thinly sliced

1. Preheat the oven to 375°F. Spray a large baking pan with olive-oil nonstick spray.

2. Place the tomatoes, onion, and garlic in a single layer on the pan. Sprinkle with the vinegar, salt, and pepper. Roast until the tomatoes are lightly browned and have an intense, sweet aroma, about 35 minutes. Remove from the oven and set aside.

3. Arrange one rack on the bottom rung of the oven. Increase the oven temperature to 500°F.

4. Sprinkle a work surface lightly with flour. Turn the dough onto the surface; knead lightly. With a lightly floured rolling pin, roll into a 12-inch circle. Transfer the circle of dough to a nonstick pizza pan or baking sheet, gently pulling the dough back to a 12-inch circle.

5. Spoon the tomato mixture onto the dough; top with half of the Parmesan cheese and bake on the bottom rack of the oven until the crust is golden and the cheese melts slightly, 12–15 minutes. Sprinkle with the remaining Parmesan cheese and the basil just before serving.

Per serving (¼ of pizza): 388 Cal, 5 g Fat, 2 g Sat Fat, 6 mg Chol, 717 mg Sod, 71 g Carb, 5 g Fib, 14 g Prot, 123 mg Calc. *POINTS: 7.*

 Shaving Parmesan is a snap with a sharp vegetable peeler. But gourmet kitchen stores carry a specially-designed gadget to make shaving cheese even easier.

Roasted Vegetable and "Soysage" Deep-Dish Pizza

Makes 12 servings

If you own a large deep-dish or Chicago-style pizza pan, you can pull it out. Otherwise, use two 9-inch round baking pans. The breakfast veggie patties, available in the frozen-food section of the supermarket, are a delicious soy-based alternative to regular sausage.

6 cups broccoli florets

3 cups corn, fresh cut from the cob or frozen, thawed

2 red or yellow bell peppers, seeded and cut into ½-inch pieces

1 large red onion, cut into 12 wedges

1½ tablespoons olive oil

1 teaspoon salt

½ teaspoon freshly ground pepper

1 recipe (about 2 pounds) Basic Pizza Dough—cornmeal variation (page 11), at room temperature

1 (8-ounce) package frozen breakfast veggie patties, cut into 1-inch pieces

1 (4-ounce) can chopped green chiles

1½ cups shredded part-skim Monterey Jack cheese

1. Arrange one rack on the bottom rung of the oven. Preheat the oven to 425°F. Spray 2 large baking pans with nonstick spray.

2. Combine the broccoli, corn, bell peppers, onion, oil, salt, and pepper in a large bowl. Spread in single layers on the 2 baking pans and roast until the vegetables are lightly browned and fragrant, 20–25 minutes, switching the pans once from top to bottom halfway through the roasting time.

3. Spray a 14-inch deep-dish pizza pan with nonstick spray. Sprinkle a work surface lightly with flour. Turn the dough onto the surface; knead lightly. With a lightly floured rolling pin, roll into a 16-inch circle. Transfer the circle to the pizza pan, gently fitting it up the sides of the pan. If using 2 (9-inch) round baking pans, cut the dough in half, roll each half into an 11-inch circle, and fit into and up the sides of the pans.

4. Arrange the roasted vegetables and the pattie pieces on the dough. Sprinkle with the chiles, then the cheese. Bake on the bottom rack of the oven until the crust is golden and the cheese melts, 25–30 minutes for the large pizza and 20–23 minutes for the 2 smaller pizzas.

Per serving (½₂ of pizza): 340 Cal, 8 g Fat, 2 g Sat Fat, 8 mg Chol, 702 mg Sod, 52 g Carb, 6 g Fib, 16 g Prot, 174 mg Calc. *POINTS: 7.*

 tip When you are fitting a large piece of rolled-out dough into a large pan, it helps to fold the dough in fourths, place it in the pan, then unfold it and fit it into the pan.

Potato and Cheddar Pizza Paysanne

Makes 6 servings

This rustic, peasant pizza makes a satisfying meal, needing only the accompaniment of a steamed fresh green, such as broccoli or string beans. Be sure to choose a waxy potato, that holds its shape well after cooking—try Yukon Gold, fingerling, or red potatoes. Avoid the starchier potato, such as a russet or baking potato, which tends to break apart after cooking.

1 pound Yukon Gold potatoes, scrubbed
1 tablespoon butter
2 bunches scallions, thinly sliced
½ teaspoon salt
¼ teaspoon freshly ground pepper
½ recipe (about 1 pound) Basic Pizza Dough—whole-wheat variation (page 11), at room temperature
1 cup shredded extra-sharp cheddar cheese
1¼ cups fat-free egg substitute

1. Bring the potatoes, with enough water to cover, to a boil in a saucepan. Reduce the heat and simmer, covered, until just tender, about 15 minutes. Drain and set aside until cool enough to handle. Cut into ¼-inch slices.
2. Melt the butter in a large nonstick skillet over medium heat, then add the scallions. Cook, stirring occasionally, until golden, 8–10 minutes. Stir in the sliced potatoes, salt, and pepper.
3. Preheat the oven to 425°F. Spray a 9-inch springform pan with nonstick spray.
4. Sprinkle a work surface lightly with flour. Turn the dough onto the surface; knead lightly. With a lightly floured rolling pin, roll into a 12-inch circle. Transfer the circle of dough to the pan, gently fitting the dough halfway up the sides of the pan.
5. Spread the potato mixture over the dough. Sprinkle with ½ cup of the cheese. Pour the egg substitute on top, then sprinkle with the remaining ½ cup cheese. Bake 15 minutes. Reduce the oven temperature to 375°F and bake until the crust is golden and a knife inserted in the center comes out clean, about 30 minutes. Remove the rim from the pan and let stand 5 minutes. Cut into wedges and serve at once.

Per serving (⅙ of pizza): 386 Cal, 10 g Fat, 5 g Sat Fat, 25 mg Chol, 739 mg Sod, 55 g Carb, 5 g Fib, 19 g Prot, 194 mg Calc. *POINTS: 8.*

Potato and Cheddar
Pizza Paysanne

Individual Salad Pizzas

Makes 6 servings

These neat pizzas, which resemble flatbreads, are topped with a mixed green salad to make a lovely light meal. Alternatively, you can serve these flatbreads as an accompaniment to any favorite entrée.

½ recipe (about 1 pound) Basic Pizza Dough— whole-wheat variation (page 11), at room temperature

4 ounces Gruyère cheese, shredded

2 tablespoons aged white-wine vinegar

1 tablespoon olive oil

½ small garlic clove, minced

1 teaspoon honey

½ teaspoon Dijon mustard

½ teaspoon ground coriander

¼ teaspoon salt

Freshly ground black pepper, to taste

8 cups mesclun salad greens

1 small apple, cored and diced

2 tablespoons chopped toasted walnuts

1. Arrange one rack on the bottom rung of the oven and another rack on the top third of the oven. Preheat the oven to 450°F.

2. Cut the dough into 6 pieces. Sprinkle a work surface lightly with flour. Turn the dough onto the surface; knead lightly. With a lightly floured rolling pin, roll each piece into a 6-inch circle. Transfer the circles of dough to 2 large nonstick baking sheets, then sprinkle with the cheese. Bake until the crusts are golden and the cheese melts, about 10 minutes, switching the pans once from top to bottom halfway through the baking time. Remove the crusts from the baking sheets and transfer to a rack to cool slightly, 2–3 minutes.

3. Combine the vinegar, oil, garlic, honey, mustard, coriander, salt, and pepper in a small bowl. Place the mesclun greens and apple in a large bowl; add the dressing and toss to coat. Spoon the salad evenly over the warm crusts, then sprinkle with the walnuts.

Per serving (1 pizza): 316 Cal, 12 g Fat, 4 g Sat Fat, 21 mg Chol, 482 mg Sod, 39 g Carb, 5 g Fib, 13 g Prot, 241 mg Calc. **POINTS: 7.**

 tip For a honey-flavored whole-wheat dough, substitute 2 teaspoons honey for the 1 teaspoon sugar in the dough recipe.

Sesame, Shallot, and Thyme Focaccia

Makes 8 servings

A focaccia is basically a thick pizza with few toppings. This one needs only a hot soup, such as a zesty minestrone or hearty chicken-vegetable, to make a hearty supper.

1 cup warm (105–115°F) water
1 teaspoon sugar
1 package active dry yeast
2½ cups all-purpose flour
2 tablespoons toasted sesame seeds
1 teaspoon salt
2 teaspoons Asian (dark) sesame oil
3 shallots, chopped
2 garlic cloves, minced
1 tablespoon cornmeal
1 tablespoon chopped fresh thyme or rosemary
2 tablespoons grated pecorino Romano cheese

1. Combine the water and sugar in a 2-cup measuring cup. Sprinkle in the yeast and let stand until foamy, about 5 minutes.

2. Combine the flour, sesame seeds, and salt in a food processor. With the machine running, scrape the yeast mixture through the feed tube; pulse about 1 minute, until the dough forms a ball. If necessary, knead briefly on a lightly floured surface until smooth and elastic.

3. Spray a large bowl with nonstick spray; put the dough in the bowl. Cover with plastic wrap and let the dough rise in a warm spot until it doubles in size, about 1 hour.

4. Heat a nonstick skillet over medium heat. Swirl in the oil, then add the shallots and garlic. Cook, stirring frequently, until golden, 6–8 minutes; set aside. Sprinkle a nonstick baking sheet with the cornmeal.

5. Punch down the dough. Sprinkle a work surface lightly with flour. Place the dough on the surface; kneading lightly. With a lightly floured rolling pin, roll into a 12-inch circle. Transfer the circle of dough to the baking sheet, gently pulling the dough back to a 12-inch circle. Dimple the dough with a wooden spoon handle, then prick all over with the tines of a fork. Spread the shallot mixture over the dough, then sprinkle with the thyme and cheese. Let rest in a warm spot, about 15 minutes. Preheat the oven to 425°F.

6. Bake the focaccia until the crust is golden and crisp around the edges, about 20 minutes. Let cool on the baking sheet about 5 minutes. To serve, slide the focaccia onto a large cutting board, then cut into 8 wedges.

Per serving (1 wedge): 185 Cal, 3 g Fat, 1 g Sat Fat, 2 mg Chol, 313 mg Sod, 34 g Carb, 2 g Fib, 6 g Prot, 33 mg Calc. *POINTS: 4.*

Greek Skillet Calzones

Makes 4 servings

Crisped, golden calzones, bursting with a savory, Greek spanakopita-like mixture of spinach, feta, and dill, and served with a lusty homemade tomato sauce, are a meal unto themselves. They are easily made in a skillet on top of the stove. Our first choice of skillet is heavy cast iron, which makes the crispiest crust. We keep with the Greek flavor theme by adding a touch of cinnamon to the tomato sauce.

1 tablespoon olive oil

1 large onion, chopped

1 (9-ounce) package leafy greens blend, or baby spinach leaves

1–2 tablespoons water

4 ounces feta cheese, crumbled

3 tablespoons chopped fresh dill

¼ teaspoon freshly ground pepper

½ recipe (about 1 pound) Basic Pizza Dough (page 10), at room temperature

1 cup Basic Tomato Sauce (page 12) or Roasted Tomato Sauce (page 13)

½ teaspoon cinnamon (optional)

1. Heat a large nonstick skillet over medium heat. Swirl in the oil, then add the onion. Cook, stirring frequently, until golden, about 8 minutes. Add the greens and the water; cook, stirring frequently, until wilted, about 5 minutes. Stir in the feta, dill, and pepper.

2. Sprinkle a work surface lightly with flour. Turn the dough onto the surface; knead lightly. Cut the dough into 4 pieces. With a lightly floured rolling pin, roll each piece into a 7-inch circle.

3. Spray a 7-inch cast-iron or nonstick skillet with nonstick spray; set over medium heat. Add 1 dough circle and cook until lightly browned, about 3 minutes on each side. Spread one-fourth of the greens mixture on the dough. Reduce the heat to low and cook until the dough is cooked through, about 3 minutes. Fold in half, slide out of the skillet, and serve at once. Or cover loosely with foil and keep warm in a slow oven while cooking the remaining calzones. Repeat with the remaining pieces of dough and greens mixture, making a total of 4 calzones.

4. Heat the tomato sauce and cinnamon (if using) in a saucepan until heated through. Serve with the calzones.

Per serving (1 calzone with ¼ cup sauce): 419 Cal, 13 g Fat, 5 g Sat Fat, 25 mg Chol, 861 mg Sod, 63 g Carb, 5 g Fib, 14 g Prot, 230 mg Calc. **POINTS: 9.**

 tip To speed up the cooking of the calzones, set up two skillets. You can use a 10-inch cast-iron or nonstick skillet as the second skillet.

Curried Vegetable Pizza

Makes 6 servings

A curry-topped pizza may sound strange. But if you think of the pizza crust as similar to an Indian flatbread, you'll soon see how curry and pizza can work together deliciously.

2 teaspoons olive oil
1 large onion, thinly sliced
2 garlic cloves, minced
2 teaspoons curry powder
4 cups cauliflower florets, thinly sliced
⅓ cup water
3 tablespoons raisins
¼ teaspoon salt
1 (8-ounce) can cannellini (white kidney) beans, rinsed and drained
1 (10-ounce) thin prebaked pizza crust
3 ounces part-skim mozzarella cheese, cubed

1. Preheat the oven to 450°F.

2. Heat a large nonstick skillet over medium-high heat. Swirl in the oil, then add the onion and garlic. Cook, stirring frequently, until softened, about 5 minutes. Stir in the curry powder and cook until fragrant, about 30 seconds.

3. Stir the cauliflower, water, raisins, and salt into the skillet. Cover and cook, stirring occasionally, until the cauliflower is crisp-tender and the raisins are plumped, about 8 minutes. Stir in the beans.

4. Place the pizza crust on a nonstick pizza pan or baking sheet. Spoon the cauliflower mixture evenly over the crust, then sprinkle with the cheese. Bake until heated through and the cheese melts and is lightly browned, about 15 minutes.

Per serving (⅙ of pizza): 234 Cal, 7 g Fat, 3 g Sat Fat, 8 mg Chol, 454 mg Sod, 34 g Carb, 4 g Fib, 11 g Prot, 245 mg Calc. *POINTS: 4.*

tip Cauliflower florets can be quite large. You'll find them more usable in a recipe such as this if you slice them first. Try slicing cauliflower florets before steaming or stir-frying them—they'll cook faster than whole florets and absorb more flavor from a sauce.

Caramelized Onion, Fig,
and Stilton Pizza

Caramelized Onion, Fig, and Stilton Pizza

Makes 6 servings

Sweet, large, and juicy, Vidalia onions are perfect for caramelizing. They hail from Vidalia, Georgia, and are mostly available from May through June. If you can't find them, substitute 6 regular yellow onions or 3 yellow and 3 red onions. In this recipe, the natural sugar from the figs also helps to sweeten and caramelize the onions. Savory, tangy Stilton is our first choice of blue cheese here, but you can substitute any good blue-vein cheese, such as Roquefort or Gorgonzola.

2 teaspoons olive oil
1 teaspoon butter
3 Vidalia onions, thinly sliced
6 dried figs, stems removed, then sliced
1 (10-ounce) thin prebaked pizza crust
3 ounces Stilton cheese, crumbled

1. To caramelize the onions, heat a 12-inch nonstick skillet over medium heat. Swirl in the oil and butter, then add the onions and cook, stirring occasionally, until light golden, about 6 minutes. Reduce the heat to low, stir in the figs, and cook, stirring occasionally, until the onions are golden brown and well softened and the figs are softened, about 12 minutes.
2. Preheat the oven to 450°F. Place the pizza crust on a nonstick pizza pan or baking sheet. Spoon the onion mixture on the crust, then sprinkle with the cheese. Bake until heated through and the cheese melts slightly, about 15 minutes.

Per serving (⅙ of pizza): 264 Cal, 10 g Fat, 5 g Sat Fat, 14 mg Chol, 450 mg Sod, 38 g Carb, 4 g Fib, 9 g Prot, 239 mg Calc. **POINTS: 5.**

 CUT POINTS Make this pizza serve eight instead of six and save almost a **POINT** per serving.

Giant Popover Portobello Pizza

Makes 4 servings

Simple popover batter forms the crust for this unusual "pizza." It's perfect for a night when you feel like pizza but don't have any pizza dough on hand. The mixed white-and-Portobello-mushroom topping provides rich flavor, and the zesty tomato sauce makes a nice accompaniment to the dish.

1 tablespoon olive oil	1. Preheat the oven to 400°F. Spray a 10-inch pie plate with nonstick spray.
4 shallots, chopped	
½ pound fresh white mushrooms, cleaned and sliced	2. Heat a large nonstick skillet over medium-high heat. Swirl in the oil, then add the shallots. Cook, stirring frequently, until golden, about 8 minutes. Add the white and Portobello mushrooms. Cook, stirring frequently, until all the liquid evaporates, 6–8 minutes. Stir in the parsley, ¼ teaspoon of the salt, and the pepper; set aside.
½ pound Portobello mushrooms, cleaned and chopped	
¼ cup chopped fresh parsley	
¾ teaspoon salt	
¼ teaspoon freshly ground pepper	3. Combine the flour and remaining ½ teaspoon salt in a medium bowl. Add the egg substitute and milk; mix until all the flour is just moistened. Pour the batter into the pie plate. Spoon the mushroom mixture over the top. Bake until the sides are puffed and lightly browned, about 20 minutes. Sprinkle with the cheese and bake until the cheese melts and is golden, 8–10 minutes.
¾ cup all-purpose flour	
½ cup fat-free egg substitute	
½ cup fat-free milk	
1 cup shredded part-skim mozzarella cheese	4. Let stand 5 minutes, then cut into 4 wedges and serve with the tomato sauce.
1⅓ cups Basic Tomato Sauce (page 12)	

Per serving (1 wedge with ⅓ cup sauce): 291 Cal, 9 g Fat, 4 g Sat Fat, 17 mg Chol, 720 mg Sod, 34 g Carb, 3 g Fib, 17 g Prot, 258 mg Calc.
POINTS: 6.

Seven-Layer Taco Pizzas

Makes 4 servings

Classic seven-layer dip shines here on its very own golden, crisped tortilla. Chipotle peppers in the chipotle salsa give a wonderful smoky flavor to the dish, but if you prefer use your favorite salsa—mild or fiery hot. For an extra ½ *POINT* per serving, top each pizza with 1½ tablespoons of light sour cream.

1 (15-ounce) can pinto beans
4 (6-inch) fat-free flour tortillas
½ cup chipotle salsa
1⅓ cups shredded romaine lettuce
½ cup shredded reduced-fat cheddar cheese
1 medium tomato, chopped
4 scallions, thinly sliced

1. Drain the pinto beans, reserving 2 tablespoons of the liquid. Rinse the beans and puree with the reserved liquid in a blender or food processor.
2. Spray a 7-inch nonstick skillet with nonstick spray and set over medium-high heat. Add 1 tortilla and cook until golden, 1–2 minutes on each side. Repeat with the remaining 3 tortillas.
3. Place a tortilla on each of 4 plates. Spread the bean puree evenly on each tortilla. Then top each evenly with the salsa, lettuce, cheese, and tomato. Sprinkle evenly with the scallions.

Per serving (1 pizza): 189 Cal, 3 g Fat, 2 g Sat Fat, 8 mg Chol, 642 mg Sod, 32 g Carb, 6 g Fib, 12 g Prot, 143 mg Calc. *POINTS: 3.*

Red Bean and Escarole Pitzas

Makes 4 servings

"Beans and greens"—in this case red beans and escarole—a favorite in vegetarian households, makes a perfect topping for pita breads. If you like, try one of the flavored pitas, such as onion or sesame. Tangy feta cheese melts on top, tying it all together.

1 tablespoon olive oil
5 garlic cloves, minced
1 bunch escarole, cleaned and shredded
1 (15-ounce) can red kidney beans, rinsed and drained
1 plum tomato, diced
1 teaspoon dried oregano
4 (6-inch) whole-wheat pita breads
4 ounces feta cheese, crumbled

1. Heat a 12-inch nonstick skillet over medium heat. Swirl in the oil, then add the garlic. Cook, stirring frequently, until fragrant and light golden, 2–3 minutes. Add the escarole, tossing to stir in the garlic. Cover and cook, stirring occasionally, until the escarole just begins to wilt, about 5 minutes.

2. Stir in the beans, tomato, and oregano. Cook, uncovered, until heated through and most of the liquid has evaporated, about 5 minutes.

3. Preheat the broiler. Place the pita breads on a baking sheet. Spoon the escarole mixture on top. Sprinkle with the feta cheese and broil until hot and the cheese is lightly browned, 3–4 minutes.

Per serving (1 pitza): 362 Cal, 12 g Fat, 5 g Sat Fat, 25 mg Chol, 774 mg Sod, 53 g Carb, 13 g Fib, 16 g Prot, 237 mg Calc. **POINTS: 7.**

 tip Be careful when cooking garlic; burned garlic has a bitter flavor and should be discarded. Remove the skillet from the heat just as the garlic begins to turn golden. The water that clings to the washed escarole leaves helps cook it. If your escarole is a little dry, add 1 to 2 tablespoons water.

Pizza Loaf

Makes 6 servings

A hollowed-out Italian bread filled with a sausage-and-pepper-like mixture makes an easy family dinner. Vegetable breakfast links can be found in the frozen-food section of the supermarket. If you prefer, substitute ½ cup textured vegetable protein for the vegetable breakfast links. Textured vegetable protein is made from soybeans and can be found in health food stores and some supermarkets.

2 teaspoons olive oil
1 onion, finely chopped
1 small green bell pepper, seeded and chopped
1 cup chopped fresh fennel or celery
1¼ cups Basic Tomato Sauce (page 12)
4 ounces frozen vegetable breakfast links, thawed and thinly sliced
¼ teaspoon salt
1 (12-ounce) semolina bread
½ cup shredded part-skim mozzarella cheese
2 tablespoons grated Parmesan cheese

1. Preheat the oven to 350°F. Line a baking sheet with foil.
2. Heat a large nonstick skillet over medium-high heat. Swirl in the oil, then add the onion, bell pepper, and fennel. Cook, stirring frequently, until softened, about 10 minutes. Stir in the tomato sauce, breakfast links, and salt. Simmer, uncovered, until heated through, 3–5 minutes.
3. Cut off the top fourth of the bread, lengthwise. Pull out the soft insides of the bread, leaving a ½-inch-thick shell. Place the shell on the baking sheet. (Save the top and soft insides of the bread to make bread crumbs for future use.)
4. Spoon the tomato sauce mixture into the bread shell. Sprinkle with the cheeses and bake until heated through and the cheeses are golden, 20–25 minutes. With a serrated knife, cut the loaf into 6 slices.

Per serving (1 slice): 189 Cal, 6 g Fat, 2 g Sat Fat, 7 mg Chol, 555 mg Sod, 23 g Carb, 3 g Fib, 11 g Prot, 138 mg Calc. ***POINTS: 4.***

 For typical sausage-and-pepper flavor, add 1 teaspoon ground fennel seeds to the tomato sauce mixture. You can easily grind fennel seeds using a coffee grinder, spice mill, or mortar and pestle.

Pizza Deluxe

Mega-Delicious Toppings

Mexican Pizza Grande

Makes 6 servings

This tasty pizza is rich with fiery Southwest flavors, and has a crunchy crust thanks to the addition of cornmeal. If you're looking for extra spice—and you can afford an extra ½ *POINT* per serving—substitute hot Italian turkey sausage for the ground turkey. For even more spice, add a sprinkling of crushed red pepper to the topping before baking.

2 teaspoons olive oil

1 onion, chopped

1 green bell pepper, seeded and chopped

2 garlic cloves, minced

½ pound ground skinless turkey breast

3 tablespoons taco seasoning mix

1 (14½-ounce) can diced tomatoes

½ cup water

2 tablespoons canned chopped mild green chiles

¼ cup sliced pitted ripe olives

½ recipe (about 1 pound) Basic Pizza Dough—cornmeal variation (page 11), at room temperature

½ cup shredded reduced-fat cheddar cheese

2 tablespoons chopped fresh cilantro

1. Arrange one rack on the bottom rung of the oven. Preheat the oven to 475°F.

2. Heat a large nonstick skillet over medium-high heat. Swirl in the oil, then add the onion, bell pepper, and garlic. Cook, stirring occasionally, until softened, about 8 minutes. Add the turkey and seasoning mix. Cook, breaking up the turkey with a fork, until the turkey begins to brown, about 6 minutes. Stir in the tomatoes, water, chiles, and olives; bring to a boil. Cook, uncovered, over medium-high heat until most of the liquid has evaporated, about 8 minutes. Remove from the heat and set aside.

3. Sprinkle a work surface lightly with flour. Turn the dough onto the surface; knead lightly. With a lightly floured rolling pin, roll into a 15-inch circle. Transfer the circle of dough to a nonstick pizza pan or large baking sheet, gently pulling the dough back to a 15-inch circle.

4. Spoon the turkey mixture onto the dough, then sprinkle with the cheese. Bake on the bottom rack of the oven until the crust is golden and the cheese melts, 15–20 minutes. Sprinkle with the cilantro just before serving.

Per serving (⅙ of pizza): 337 Cal, 7 g Fat, 2 g Sat Fat, 28 mg Chol, 791 mg Sod, 50 g Carb, 4 g Fib, 18 g Prot, 128 mg Calc. *POINTS: 7.*

Roasted Onion and Olive Pizza with Goat Cheese

Makes 6 servings

Onions and garlic develop a wonderfully sweet and mellow flavor when roasted. They are not only delicious as a pizza topping, but equally good in sandwiches or spooned over sautéed chicken or meat.

1 large red onion, cut into
½-inch-thick wedges
6 whole shallots, cut
lengthwise in half
6 garlic cloves, cut in half
½ teaspoon salt
½ teaspoon freshly ground
pepper
½ teaspoon dried thyme
½ recipe (about 1 pound)
Basic Pizza Dough—
semolina variation
(page 11), at room
temperature
15 oil-cured black olives,
pitted and chopped
3 ounces reduced-fat goat
cheese
¼ cup chopped fresh basil

1. Preheat the oven to 400°F. Spray a large baking pan with olive-oil nonstick spray.
2. Place the onion, shallots, and garlic in a single layer on the pan. Sprinkle with the salt, pepper, and thyme. Lightly spray the vegetables with olive-oil nonstick spray. Roast until tender and lightly browned, about 20 minutes. Remove from the oven and set aside.
3. Arrange one rack on the bottom rung of the oven. Increase the oven temperature to 450°F.
4. Sprinkle a work surface lightly with flour. Turn the dough onto the surface; knead lightly. With a lightly floured rolling pin, roll into a 12-inch circle. Transfer the circle of dough to a nonstick pizza pan or baking sheet, gently pulling the dough back to a 12-inch circle.
5. Spoon the roasted onion mixture on the dough; top with the olives and goat cheese. Bake on the bottom rack of the oven until the crust is golden and the cheese is slightly melted, about 15 minutes. Sprinkle with the basil just before serving.

Per serving (⅙ of pizza): 252 Cal, 6 g Fat, 3 g Sat Fat, 13 mg Chol, 627 mg Sod, 42 g Carb, 3 g Fib, 8 g Prot, 120 mg Calc. **POINTS: 5.**

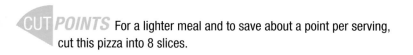

CUT POINTS For a lighter meal and to save about a point per serving, cut this pizza into 8 slices.

Pizza Primavera

Pizza Primavera

Makes 6 servings

Veggie lovers will adore this pizza, so chock-full of fresh spring bounty. The colorful asparagus, zucchini, and yellow squash are roasted to intensify their flavors. Substitute other vegetables, such as chunks of eggplant or small broccoli florets, if you like.

½ pound fresh asparagus, trimmed and cut into 3-inch pieces

2 plum tomatoes, cut into ¾-inch chunks

1 zucchini, cut into ¾-inch chunks

1 yellow squash, cut into ¾-inch chunks

1 red onion, cut into ¾-inch chunks

1 tablespoon extra-virgin olive oil

½ teaspoon salt

½ teaspoon freshly ground pepper

½ recipe (about 1 pound) Basic Pizza Dough (page 10), at room temperature

¾ cup shredded part-skim mozzarella cheese

¼ cup chopped fresh basil

1 (1-ounce) piece Parmesan cheese, shaved

1. Preheat the oven to 450°F. Spray a large baking pan with olive-oil nonstick spray.
2. Combine the asparagus, tomatoes, zucchini, yellow squash, red onion, oil, salt, and pepper in a large bowl; toss to coat. Place the vegetables in a single layer on the pan. Roast until tender and lightly browned, 20–25 minutes. Remove the pan from the oven and set aside.
3. Arrange one rack on the bottom rung of the oven. Increase the oven temperature to 475°F.
4. Sprinkle a work surface lightly with flour. Turn the dough onto the surface; knead lightly. With a lightly floured rolling pin, roll into a 12-inch circle. Transfer the circle of dough to a nonstick pizza pan or baking sheet, gently pulling the dough back to a 12-inch circle.
5. Sprinkle the dough with the mozzarella cheese, then top with the roasted vegetables. Bake on the bottom rack of the oven until the crust is golden and the cheese melts, about 25 minutes. Sprinkle with the basil and Parmesan cheese just before serving.

Per serving (⅙ of pizza): 268 Cal, 7 g Fat, 3 g Sat Fat, 9 mg Chol, 629 mg Sod, 40 g Carb, 3 g Fib, 11 g Prot, 164 mg Calc. *POINTS: 5.*

 tip Fresh Parmesan cheese shavings are easy to make. Simply use a vegetable peeler in a downward motion to peel off thin strips from a block of Parmesan (1 ounce makes about ¼ cup of shavings). Do this right before serving, or refrigerate the shavings until ready to use.

Pesto Pizza with Roasted Yellow Peppers and Tomatoes

Makes 6 servings

Roasted yellow peppers add color and a bright, sweet taste to this pizza. Find them packed in jars in your supermarket alongside the roasted red peppers. If you can't find roasted yellow peppers, try roasting your own, or use a jar of roasted red peppers.

½ cup lightly packed fresh
  basil leaves

1 tablespoon pine nuts

2 tablespoons grated
  Parmesan cheese

2 teaspoons extra-virgin
  olive oil

1 small garlic clove,
  chopped

2 teaspoons water

½ recipe (about 1 pound)
  Basic Pizza Dough (page
  10), at room temperature

⅔ cup grape tomatoes
  (about 16 tomatoes),
  halved

4 roasted yellow peppers,
  cut into thin strips (about
  1⅓ cups)

2 ounces reduced-fat feta
  cheese, crumbled (about
  ½ cup)

2 tablespoons chopped
  fresh oregano

1. To make the pesto, combine the basil, pine nuts, 1 tablespoon of the Parmesan cheese, the oil, and garlic in a blender or food processor. Puree to a coarse paste. With the machine running, gradually add the water and mix to a smooth paste; transfer to a small bowl and set aside.

2. Arrange one rack on the bottom rung of the oven. Preheat the oven to 450°F.

3. Sprinkle a work surface lightly with flour. Turn the dough onto the surface; knead lightly. With a lightly floured rolling pin, roll into a 12-inch circle. Transfer the circle of dough to a nonstick pizza pan or baking sheet, gently pulling the dough back to a 12-inch circle.

4. Spread the reserved pesto over the dough. Top with the tomatoes, yellow peppers, and feta cheese. Bake on the bottom rack of the oven until the crust is golden and the cheese melts, 12–15 minutes. Sprinkle with the oregano and the remaining 1 tablespoon Parmesan cheese just before serving.

Per serving (⅙ of pizza): 240 Cal, 6 g Fat, 2 g Sat Fat, 10 mg Chol, 343 mg Sod, 40 g Carb, 3 g Fib, 8 g Prot, 100 mg Calc. ***POINTS: 5.***

 tip Make a double or triple batch of the pesto and freeze the extra in ice cube trays, then transfer the frozen cubes to a zip-close plastic freezer bag to use another time. Or substitute ¼ cup prepared pesto, found in jars in the refrigerator case of most supermarkets.

Spanakopizza

Makes 6 servings

This delicious stuffed pizza has a filling similar to that in the classic Greek spinach pie, spanakopita. If you prefer, use an 8-ounce bag of fresh spinach instead of frozen. For milder flavor, substitute ⅓ cup reduced-fat mild goat cheese or 3 ounces light cream cheese (Neufchâtel) for the feta cheese.

2 teaspoons canola oil

1 onion, chopped

1 (10-ounce) package frozen chopped spinach, thawed and squeezed dry

1 cup fat-free ricotta cheese

⅓ cup reduced-fat feta cheese, crumbled

¼ cup chopped fresh dill

4 scallions, thinly sliced

½ teaspoon freshly ground pepper

½ recipe (about 1 pound) Basic Pizza Dough— whole-wheat variation (page 11), at room temperature

1. Arrange one rack on the bottom rung of the oven. Preheat the oven to 450°F.

2. Heat a large nonstick skillet over medium-high heat. Swirl in the oil, then add the onion. Cook, stirring frequently, until the onion is tender, about 6 minutes. If the onion seems too dry, add ¼ cup water and cook, stirring frequently, until the water has evaporated, about 3 minutes. Stir in the spinach and cook, stirring frequently, until the flavors are blended, about 3 minutes. Transfer the onion mixture to a large bowl. Stir in the ricotta cheese, feta cheese, dill, scallions, and pepper until well blended.

3. Sprinkle a work surface lightly with flour. Turn the dough onto the surface; cut the dough into 2 pieces. Knead each piece lightly, then with a lightly floured rolling pin, roll each into a 12-inch circle. Transfer one circle of dough to a nonstick pizza pan or baking sheet, and gently pull the dough back to a 12-inch circle.

4. Spoon the spinach mixture on the dough, spreading the mixture to 1 inch from the edge. Brush the edge with water. Place the second circle of dough on top and crimp the edges to seal. Cut 4 (2-inch) slashes on top. Bake on the bottom rack of the oven until the filling is hot and the crust is golden, about 25 minutes.

Per serving (⅙ of pie): 250 Cal, 4 g Fat, 1 g Sat Fat, 7 mg Chol, 154 mg Sod, 41 g Carb, 4 g Fib, 13 g Prot, 175 mg Calc. *POINTS: 5.*

Pizza with Caramelized Leeks

Pizza with Caramelized Leeks

Makes 6 servings

Caramelizing vegetables simply involves cooking them slowly over medium-low heat until they're very tender and golden brown. Leeks are perfect for this technique. Ready-to-bake pizza crusts are partially baked and come in a variety of sizes. Here we use one (12-inch) crust from a two-crust (16-ounce) package, found in the refrigerator section of most supermarkets. Use a 10-ounce prebaked thin pizza crust if you prefer.

2 tablespoons butter
1½ pounds leeks, trimmed and cleaned
½ cup water
1 teaspoon sugar
¼ teaspoon salt
2 shallots, thinly sliced
1 garlic clove, minced
1 (12-inch) ready-to-bake pizza crust
2 small tomatoes, thinly sliced
½ cup shredded light Jarlsberg cheese
1 tablespoon chopped fresh thyme

1. Heat a large nonstick skillet over medium heat. Swirl in the butter, then add the leeks, water, sugar, and salt; bring to a boil. Reduce the heat and simmer, covered, stirring occasionally, until the leeks have browned and the liquid has evaporated, about 15 minutes. Add the shallots and garlic. Cook, uncovered, until the shallots are soft, about 5 minutes. Set aside to cool.

2. Arrange one rack on the bottom rung of the oven. Preheat the oven to 450°F.

3. Place the pizza crust on a nonstick pizza pan or baking sheet. Spoon the leek mixture evenly over the crust. Arrange the tomatoes on top, then sprinkle with the cheese. Bake on the bottom rack of the oven until the crust is golden and the cheese melts, 20–25 minutes. Sprinkle with the thyme just before serving.

Per serving (⅙ of pizza): 194 Cal, 8 g Fat, 4 g Sat Fat, 15 mg Chol, 357 mg Sod, 25 g Carb, 3 g Fib, 7 g Prot, 123 mg Calc. **POINTS: 4.**

 tip Leeks are often quite sandy, so be sure to clean them well. To do this, trim away most of the dark green tops and the roots, leaving the root end intact to hold the layers together. Slice the leek lengthwise to within a half inch of the root end. Hold the leeks by the root end, fan open the layers, and rinse thoroughly under cold running water.

Greek Salad Pizza with Creamy Feta Dressing

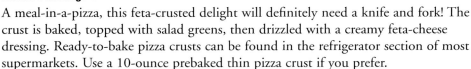

Makes 8 servings

A meal-in-a-pizza, this feta-crusted delight will definitely need a knife and fork! The crust is baked, topped with salad greens, then drizzled with a creamy feta-cheese dressing. Ready-to-bake pizza crusts can be found in the refrigerator section of most supermarkets. Use a 10-ounce prebaked thin pizza crust if you prefer.

¼ cup low-fat mayonnaise
¼ cup light sour cream
2 tablespoons + ⅓ cup crumbled reduced-fat feta cheese
1 tablespoon low-fat (1%) milk
1 tablespoon lemon juice
1 tablespoon chopped dill
3 cups torn romaine lettuce
½ green bell pepper, seeded and finely chopped
½ cucumber, peeled, seeded and finely chopped
1 small tomato, chopped
1 red onion, thinly sliced
8 oil-cured black olives, pitted and halved
2 teaspoons olive oil
2 (6-ounce) bags fresh baby spinach
2 garlic cloves, minced
1 (12-inch) ready-to-bake pizza crust

1. To make the dressing, whisk together the mayonnaise, sour cream, the 2 tablespoons feta cheese, the milk, lemon juice, and dill in a small bowl. Cover and refrigerate until ready to use.

2. Combine the lettuce, bell pepper, cucumber, tomato, onion, and olives in a large bowl. Cover with damp paper towels and set aside.

3. Arrange one rack on the bottom rung of the oven. Preheat the oven to 450°F.

4. Heat a medium nonstick skillet over medium-high heat. Swirl in the oil, then add the spinach and garlic. Cook, stirring occasionally, until the spinach just begins to wilt, about 3 minutes.

5. Place the pizza crust on a nonstick pizza pan or baking sheet. Spoon the spinach mixture onto the pizza crust. Top with the remaining ⅓ cup feta cheese. Bake on the bottom rack of the oven until the crust is golden and crisp and the cheese begins to melt, about 10 minutes. Slide the pizza onto a large cutting board. Top the pizza with the lettuce mixture, then drizzle with the dressing.

Per serving (⅛ of pizza): 162 Cal, 6 g Fat, 2 g Sat Fat, 10 mg Chol, 391 mg Sod, 23 g Carb, 3 g Fib, 6 g Prot, 114 mg Calc. *POINTS: 3.*

tip Double the feta dressing and use the extra on sandwiches, over a burger, or on grilled chicken.

Chicken Chipotle Pizza

Makes 6 servings

Chipotles are smoked jalapeño peppers. Chipotles en adobo come in 7-ounce cans and add hot, smoky flavor to foods. You can find them in Latin American markets and some large supermarkets. Keep unused chipotles in a covered container in the refrigerator for up to three months. Ready-to-bake pizza crusts are partially baked and come in a variety of sizes. Here we use two (9-inch) crusts from a four-crust (13-ounce) package, found in the refrigerator section of the supermarket.

2 teaspoons canola oil
1 onion, sliced
1 pound skinless boneless chicken thighs, trimmed of all visible fat and cut into strips
¼ teaspoon salt
¾ cup bottled steak sauce
2 tablespoons honey
2 chipotles en adobo, chopped
2 (9-inch) ready-to-bake pizza crusts
½ cup shredded reduced-fat cheddar cheese
2 tablespoons whole cilantro leaves

1. Heat a large nonstick saucepan over medium-high heat. Swirl in the oil, then add the onion. Cook, stirring frequently, until tender, about 8 minutes.

2. Add the chicken and salt. Cook, over medium-high heat, until the chicken is browned, about 5 minutes. Add the steak sauce, honey, and chipotles. Reduce the heat and simmer, covered, until the chicken is tender and cooked through, about 15 minutes. Remove the cover and continue cooking over medium-high heat until the sauce thickens slightly, about 5 minutes. Remove from the heat and let cool slightly.

3. Arrange one rack on the bottom rung of the oven. Preheat the oven to 450°F.

4. Place the pizza crusts on a large nonstick baking sheet. Spread the chicken mixture on the crusts. Sprinkle evenly with the cheese. Bake on the bottom rack of the oven until the crusts are golden and the cheese melts, 10–12 minutes. Sprinkle with the cilantro, then cut each pizza into thirds.

Per serving (⅓ of one pizza): 336 Cal, 11 g Fat, 3 g Sat Fat, 56 mg Chol, 933 mg Sod, 36 g Carb, 2 g Fib, 23 g Prot, 99 mg Calc. **POINTS: 7.**

 CUT POINTS Use ¾ pound skinless boneless chicken breasts instead of the 1 pound skinless boneless chicken thighs and save about a **POINT** per serving.

Pizza Rustica

Makes 16 servings

This is great to take on a picnic, bring to a potluck supper, or for a hearty family meal. Make it a day ahead—it's even better the next day.

CRUST:
- 2 cups all-purpose flour
- 2 tablespoons sugar
- 2 teaspoons baking powder
- ½ teaspoon salt
- 2 tablespoons chilled unsalted butter, chopped
- ½ cup fat-free egg substitute
- ¼ cup olive oil

FILLING:
- 1 (15-ounce) container part-skim ricotta cheese
- 1 cup shredded part-skim mozzarella cheese
- 1 cup fat-free egg substitute
- 4 ounces sliced turkey pepperoni, chopped
- 4 ounces lean Canadian bacon, chopped
- ¼ cup grated Parmesan
- 2 tablespoons chopped fresh parsley
- ½ teaspoon ground pepper
- 2 tablespoons low-fat (1%) milk

1. To prepare the crust, combine the flour, sugar, baking powder, and salt in a food processor; pulse briefly to mix. Add the butter and pulse until the mixture resembles coarse crumbs. With the machine running, add the egg substitute and oil; pulse until the dough forms a ball, about 30 seconds. Cut the dough in half; shape each half into a disk. Cover and refrigerate to chill, about 30 minutes.

2. To prepare the filling, drain the ricotta; mix with the mozzarella, egg substitute, pepperoni, bacon, Parmesan cheese, parsley, and pepper in a food processor. Pulse until the mixture is smooth, about 10 seconds; set aside. Preheat the oven to 350°F. Spray a 10-inch springform pan with nonstick spray.

3. On a lightly floured surface, roll one disk of dough into a 10-inch circle. Place the dough in the bottom of the pan. Spoon the filling onto the crust. Roll the remaining dough into an 11-inch circle, then cut the dough into 12 strips. Arrange half of the strips diagonally across the filling. Arrange the remaining strips diagonally across the first ones. Brush the strips with the milk. Trim the excess dough even with the rim of the pan. Bake until a knife inserted in the center comes out clean and the crust is golden, about 45 minutes. Let the pizza cool in the pan on a rack 30 minutes. Refrigerate until chilled, at least 4 hours or overnight.

4. Run a small knife around the edge of the pan. Remove the rim from the pan, then let the pizza stand at room temperature about 15 minutes before serving.

Per serving (¹⁄₁₆ of pie): 204 Cal, 10 g Fat, 4 g Sat Fat, 25 mg Chol, 437 mg Sod, 16 g Carb, 1 g Fib, 12 g Prot, 194 mg Calc. *POINTS: 5.*

Pizza Rustica

Mediterranean Pan Pizza

Makes 6 servings

A cast-iron skillet with a light spray of oil, fresh pizza dough, and some serious heat makes for the crispiest of pizza crusts. The dough puffs up beautifully in the skillet in the oven. If you don't have a 12-inch cast-iron skillet, use a deep-dish pizza pan instead.

½ pound eggplant, cut into 1-inch chunks

1 zucchini, cut into 1-inch chunks

1 plum tomato, seeded and cut into 1-inch chunks

1 tablespoon extra-virgin olive oil

½ teaspoon salt

½ teaspoon freshly ground pepper

½ recipe (about 1 pound) Basic Pizza Dough (page 10), at room temperature

1 cup Basic Tomato Sauce (page 12) or Roasted Tomato Sauce (page 13)

½ cup shredded light Havarti cheese

3 tablespoons thinly sliced fresh basil

1 tablespoon grated Parmesan cheese

1. Preheat the oven to 450°F. Spray a large roasting pan with olive-oil nonstick spray.

2. Combine the eggplant, zucchini, tomato, oil, salt, and pepper in a large bowl; toss to coat. Spread the vegetables in one layer in the roasting pan. Roast, stirring occasionally, until tender and browned, 20–25 minutes. Set aside to cool.

3. Spray a 12-inch cast-iron skillet or 12-inch deep-dish pizza pan with olive-oil nonstick spray. Arrange one rack on the bottom rung of the oven.

4. Sprinkle a work surface lightly with flour. Turn the dough onto the surface; knead lightly. With a lightly floured rolling pin, roll into a 13-inch circle. Transfer the circle of dough to the skillet, gently pulling and stretching the dough halfway up the sides of the skillet. Spray the top of the dough with olive-oil nonstick spray. Bake on the bottom rack of the oven until the dough begins to puff up slightly and the bottom just begins to brown (use a narrow metal spatula to lift the bottom of the dough to check for browning), about 20 minutes.

5. Spoon the tomato sauce on the dough; top with the roasted vegetables, then sprinkle with the Havarti cheese. Bake until the crust is golden and the cheese melts, 12–15 minutes. Sprinkle with the basil and Parmesan cheese just before serving.

Per serving (⅙ of pizza): 258 Cal, 6 g Fat, 2 g Sat Fat, 6 mg Chol, 805 mg Sod, 42 g Carb, 3 g Fib, 9 g Prot, 107 mg Calc. **POINTS: 5.**

Garlicky Potato and Caramelized Onion Pan Pizza

Makes 6 servings

The crust on this pizza is crisped to a T in a dark, heavy cast-iron skillet. The sweet, caramelized whole onions pair well with the buttery, moist flavor of Yukon Gold potatoes—we leave their skins on for extra flavor and fiber.

¾ pound Yukon Gold potatoes, cut into ½-inch-thick slices

½ teaspoon salt

3 tablespoons chopped fresh basil

2 garlic cloves, finely chopped

½ teaspoon freshly ground pepper

1 tablespoon unsalted butter

½ (1-pound) bag frozen small whole onions

½ cup water

¼ teaspoon sugar

½ recipe (about 1 pound) Basic Pizza Dough (page 10), at room temperature

1 tablespoon grated Parmesan cheese

1. Bring the potatoes, salt, and enough water to cover to a boil in a large saucepan. Reduce the heat and simmer, covered, until fork-tender, about 15 minutes; drain. Transfer the potatoes to a large bowl. Add 2 tablespoons of the basil, the garlic, and pepper; toss gently.

2. Heat the butter in a medium nonstick skillet over medium heat. Add the onions, water, and sugar. Simmer, covered, stirring occasionally, until the onions are browned and the liquid evaporates, about 15 minutes.

3. Arrange one rack on the bottom rung of the oven. Preheat the oven to 450°F. Spray a 12-inch cast-iron skillet or deep-dish pizza pan with olive-oil nonstick spray.

4. Sprinkle a work surface lightly with flour. Turn the dough onto the surface; knead lightly. With a lightly floured rolling pin, roll into a 12-inch circle. Transfer the circle of dough to the skillet, gently pulling the dough to fit halfway up the sides of the skillet. Spray the top of the dough lightly with olive-oil nonstick spray. Bake on the bottom rack of the oven until the dough puffs up slightly and the bottom just begins to brown, about 20 minutes.

5. Arrange the potatoes on the dough; top with the onion mixture and sprinkle with the cheese. Bake until hot and the cheese is lightly browned, 25–30 minutes. Sprinkle with the remaining 1 tablespoon basil just before serving.

Per serving (⅙ of pizza): 263 Cal, 4 g Fat, 2 g Sat Fat, 6 mg Chol, 373 mg Sod, 50 g Carb, 3 g Fib, 7 g Prot, 40 mg Calc. *POINTS: 5.*

tip There's no need to thaw the frozen whole onions before using them in this pizza.

Three-Mushroom, Onion, and Bacon Pizza

Makes 6 servings

Mushrooms lovers stop right here! This thin-crust pizza is loaded with flavorful, meaty white, shiitake, and Portobello mushrooms, then topped with a touch of crisp bacon and flavorful cheddar cheese.

2 teaspoons olive oil
1 cup sliced fresh white mushrooms
1 cup sliced fresh shiitake mushroom caps
1 cup sliced fresh Portobello mushroom caps
1 large onion, sliced
½ teaspoon freshly ground pepper
¼ teaspoon salt
¼ cup dry white wine
1 tablespoon chopped fresh thyme
1 (10-ounce) package thin prebaked pizza crust
4 slices bacon, crisp-cooked, drained, and crumbled
½ cup shredded reduced-fat cheddar cheese

1. Preheat the oven to 450°F.
2. Heat a large nonstick skillet over medium-high heat. Swirl in the oil, then add the mushrooms, onion, pepper, and salt. Cook, stirring frequently, until the mushrooms and onion are very tender, about 15 minutes. Add the wine and simmer, uncovered, until the liquid has evaporated, about 3 minutes. Remove from the heat and stir in the thyme.
3. Place the pizza crust on a pizza pan or baking sheet. Spoon the mushroom mixture onto the crust. Sprinkle with the bacon, then the cheese. Bake until heated through and the cheese is lightly browned, about 15 minutes.

Per serving (⅙ of pizza): 217 Cal, 8 g Fat, 2 g Sat Fat, 9 mg Chol, 436 mg Sod, 27 g Carb, 2 g Fib, 8 g Prot, 85 mg Calc. **POINTS: 5.**

 tip Try turkey bacon here—it makes a great lean substitute for regular bacon. To keep it moist, avoid overcooking it.

Spicy Broccoli and Sun-Dried Tomato Pizza

Makes 6 servings

Broccoli, often a favorite in Chinese dishes because it absorbs so many of the fabulous flavors, works wonders here—with the help of pungent garlic and spicy crushed red pepper.

4 cups fresh broccoli florets
12 sun-dried tomatoes (not oil-packed)
2 teaspoons olive oil
4 garlic cloves, chopped
¼ teaspoon crushed red pepper
¼ teaspoon salt
1 (10-ounce) package thin prebaked pizza crust
1 cup Basic Tomato Sauce (page 12) or Roasted Tomato Sauce (page 13)
1 cup shredded part-skim mozzarella cheese

1. Bring a pot of lightly salted water to a boil. Add the broccoli and return to a boil. Cook until just crisp-tender, about 5 minutes. Drain, reserving 1 cup of the cooking liquid.

2. Pour the reserved 1 cup cooking liquid over the sun-dried tomatoes in a small bowl. Let stand until the tomatoes are softened, about 15 minutes. Drain, then cut the tomatoes into thin strips.

3. Preheat the oven to 450°F.

4. Heat a large nonstick skillet over medium heat. Swirl in the oil, then add the garlic and crushed red pepper. Cook, stirring frequently, until the garlic just begins to turn golden, about 2 minutes. Add the broccoli, sun-dried tomatoes, and salt. Cook, stirring occasionally, until the flavors are blended, about 5 minutes.

5. Place the pizza crust on a pizza pan or baking sheet. Spoon the broccoli mixture evenly over the crust. Top with the tomato sauce, then sprinkle with the cheese. Bake until heated through and the cheese melts, 12–15 minutes.

Per serving (⅙ of pizza): 248 Cal, 8 g Fat, 3 g Sat Fat, 10 mg Chol, 817 mg Sod, 33 g Carb, 4 g Fib, 11 g Prot, 183 mg Calc. *POINTS: 5.*

 tip Although the taste of the fresh is far superior, you can use frozen broccoli spears or frozen chopped broccoli instead. Be sure to cook the frozen broccoli according to package directions, then drain it well before adding it to the garlic mixture.

Flatbread with Sausage and Peppers

Flatbread with Sausage and Peppers

Makes 6 servings

Lavash, a Middle Eastern flatbread, comes in a variety of sizes and textures, from small crisp crackers to large soft rounds, which are sometimes called mountain bread or shepherd's bread. Lavash can be found in Middle Eastern markets and some supermarkets.

2 (9-inch) whole-wheat lavash (flatbreads)
2 teaspoons olive oil
1 onion, thinly sliced
1 green bell pepper, seeded and thinly sliced
½ pound sweet Italian turkey sausage, casings removed
1 cup Basic Tomato Sauce (page 12) or Roasted Tomato Sauce (page 13)
1 cup shredded reduced-fat cheddar cheese
2 tablespoons pickled jalapeño slices, coarsely chopped

1. Heat a large nonstick skillet over medium-high heat. Add one lavash and cook, turning occasionally, until crisp and golden, about 4 minutes. Repeat with the remaining lavash. Set the lavash aside and wipe the skillet clean.

2. Preheat the oven to 450°F.

3. Heat the same skillet over medium-high heat. Swirl in the oil, then add the onion and bell pepper. Cook, stirring frequently, until the vegetables are soft, about 8 minutes. Add the sausage and cook, stirring occasionally, until the sausage is browned and the vegetables are very tender, 6–8 minutes. Stir in the tomato sauce; heat through.

4. Place the lavash on a large nonstick baking sheet. Divide the sausage mixture between the 2 lavash; spread smooth. Sprinkle evenly with the cheese and jalapeños. Bake until hot and the cheese melts, 8–10 minutes. Cut each lavash in thirds and serve at once.

Per serving (⅓ of one lavash): 203 Cal, 9 g Fat, 3 g Sat Fat, 31 mg Chol, 758 mg Sod, 18 g Carb, 3 g Fib, 14 g Prot, 179 mg Calc. *POINTS: 4.*

 tip If you prefer, you can spread the sausage mixture evenly on six rectangular flat crisp breads instead of the two 9-inch lavash and bake for only 2 to 3 minutes.

Pastrami Reuben Calzones

Makes 8 servings

The owner of the once-famous Reuben's of New York City created this sandwich classic—a combination of corned beef, sauerkraut, and Swiss cheese, drizzled with Russian dressing. We use turkey pastrami (instead of corned beef) and lean versions of the other ingredients, then tuck them into turnover-shaped pizzas (calzones).

2 teaspoons canola oil

1 onion, chopped

1 Granny Smith apple, peeled, cored, and chopped

2 cups well-drained canned sauerkraut, rinsed and squeezed dry

½ cup water

2 teaspoons caraway seeds

2 tablespoons ketchup

1 tablespoon fat-free mayonnaise

1 tablespoon sweet pickle relish

½ recipe (about 1 pound) Basic Pizza Dough (page 10), at room temperature

4 teaspoons spicy brown mustard

½ pound turkey pastrami, thinly sliced

½ cup shredded light Jarlsberg cheese

1 egg white, lightly beaten

1. Heat a large nonstick skillet over medium-high heat. Swirl in the oil, then add the onion. Cook, stirring frequently, until the onion is very tender, about 6 minutes. Add the apple and cook until the apple is tender and just begins to brown, about 5 minutes. Stir in the sauerkraut, the water, and 1 teaspoon of the caraway seeds; bring to a boil. Reduce the heat and simmer, covered, until the liquid has evaporated and the flavors are blended, about 20 minutes. Set aside to cool slightly.

2. To make the dressing, combine the ketchup, mayonnaise, and relish in a small bowl. Cover and refrigerate until ready to use. Arrange one rack on the bottom rung of the oven. Preheat the oven to 450°F.

3. Sprinkle a work surface lightly with flour. Turn the dough onto the surface; cut the dough into 4 pieces. Knead each piece lightly, then with a lightly floured rolling pin, roll each into a 6-inch circle. Spread each circle with 1 teaspoon of the mustard. Mound one-fourth of the sauerkraut mixture on half of each circle, then top each evenly with the pastrami, cheese, and dressing. Brush the edges lightly with water. Fold the dough over the filling; crimp the edges to seal.

4. Brush the top of each calzone with the egg white and sprinkle with the remaining 1 teaspoon caraway seeds. Transfer the calzones to a large nonstick baking sheet. With a sharp knife, make 3 (1-inch) slashes on top of each. Bake on the bottom rack of the oven until golden, about 20 minutes. Cut each calzone in half.

Per serving (½ calzone): 239 Cal, 6 g Fat, 2 g Sat Fat, 19 mg Chol, 1053 mg Sod, 35 g Carb, 3 g Fib, 12 g Prot, 86 mg Calc. *POINTS: 5.*

Pizza Timeline

Today pizza is as American as baseball and apple pie, but its origins tell a different story.

- Ancient Greece: **A precursor to pizza**—called "pitta," a flat unleavened bread seasoned with herbs and oil—is introduced by the Greeks to Naples and surrounding regions.

- Early 16th Century: **Spanish Conquistadors bring tomatoes to Europe** from Mexico and South America. Europeans are initially suspicious and think tomatoes are poisonous.

- Late 1600s: **Peasants from Naples are first to add tomatoes to pizza.**

- 1830: Antica Pizzeria Port'Alba, **the world's first pizzeria, opens in Naples.** These pizzas are baked in ovens lined with lava from nearby Mount Vesuvius.

- 1889: Rafaele Esposito of Naples prepares a **special pizza to honor Queen Margarita,** called Pizza Margarita. It features a fresh tomato, mozzarella, and basil topping to symbolize the red, white, and green colors of the Italian flag.

- 1905: Italian immigrant Gennaro Lombardi opens the **first pizzeria in the United States,** Lombardi's, in New York City.

- 1945: World War II GIs returning from Italy start a **nationwide demand for pizza.**

- 1950s: **Packaged pizzas begin to appear in grocery stores;** mass-production pizza chains arrive to satisfy the growing American market.

- Today: **Pizza ranks as one of the top three foods consumed in the United States.**

Pizzas Off the Grill

Crisp Pies with a Smoky Touch

Steak Lovers' Grilled Pizza

Steak Lovers' Grilled Pizza

Makes 6 servings

Grilled flank steak (sliced very thin) and onion (sliced quite thick) make a basic but excellent pizza topping. Just a dab of a soft spreading herbed cheese—such as Boursin, well seasoned with garlic, herbs, and cracked black pepper—adds a hefty dose of flavor.

1 large garlic clove
¾ teaspoon salt
¼ teaspoon freshly ground pepper
½ pound flank steak
2 medium onions, cut into ½-inch-thick slices
1 large tomato, cut into ½-inch wedges
Cornmeal, for sprinkling
½ recipe (about 1 pound) Basic Pizza Dough (page 10), at room temperature
¼ cup light herb-seasoned soft spreading cheese

1. Chop the garlic, salt, and pepper to a paste on a board. Rub both sides of the steak with the paste. Place in a zip-close plastic bag and refrigerate, about 1 hour.

2. Spray the grill rack with nonstick spray; prepare the grill for indirect cooking (see page 138). Remove the steak from the bag. Grill the steak over direct heat, about 4 minutes on each side for medium-rare. Transfer the steak to a board, let stand 10 minutes, then cut into thin slices.

3. Lightly spray the onions with nonstick spray. Grill over direct heat until lightly charred and almost tender, 4–5 minutes on each side. Wrap the onions in foil to help tenderize them, about 10 minutes. Grill the tomato wedges until light grill marks appear, about 1 minute.

4. Lightly sprinkle a large baking sheet with cornmeal. Sprinkle a work surface lightly with flour. Turn the dough onto the surface; knead lightly. With a lightly floured rolling pin, roll into a 12-inch circle. Transfer the circle to the baking sheet, gently pulling the dough back to a 12-inch circle. Slide the crust onto the direct-heat section of the grill. Cover the grill and cook until the crust is firm and light grill marks are formed, 2–3 minutes.

5. Flip the crust with tongs, then drag to the indirect-heat section of the grill. Quickly spread the cheese over the crust. Top evenly with the steak slices, onions, and tomato, leaving a ½-inch border. Return the pizza to the direct-heat section of the grill. Cover the grill and cook until the toppings are hot and the bottom is golden, 3–5 minutes. Grab the edge of the pizza with tongs, then slide onto a board.

Per serving (⅙ of pizza): 278 Cal, 6 g Fat, 2 g Sat Fat, 25 mg Chol, 662 mg Sod, 40 g Carb, 2 g Fib, 15 g Prot, 34 mg Calc. **POINTS: 6.**

Sage Chicken and Pepper Pizza

Makes 6 servings

Fresh sage, chicken, and colorful bell peppers make a great pizza topping here.

4 (4-ounce) skinless boneless chicken thighs, trimmed of all visible fat

2 tablespoons finely chopped fresh sage

2 large garlic cloves, finely chopped

1 teaspoon salt

1 large yellow bell pepper, halved and seeded

1 large red bell pepper, halved and seeded

Cornmeal, for sprinkling

½ recipe (about 1 pound) Basic Pizza Dough— cornmeal variation (page 11), at room temperature

⅓ cup part-skim shredded mozzarella cheese

1. Combine the chicken, sage, garlic, and ½ teaspoon of the salt in a zip-close plastic bag; rub the seasonings onto the chicken by pressing on the outside of the bag. Squeeze out the air and seal the bag; refrigerate 1 hour.

2. Spray the grill rack with nonstick spray; prepare the grill for indirect cooking (see page 138). Grill the peppers over direct heat until lightly charred and tender, 8–10 minutes on each side. Wrap in foil and let stand until cool enough to handle, about 15 minutes. Peel and cut into ½-inch strips; toss with the remaining ½ teaspoon salt. Meanwhile, remove the chicken from the bag, then grill over direct heat until cooked through, 4–5 minutes on each side. Coarsely chop the chicken.

3. Lightly sprinkle a large baking sheet with cornmeal. Turn the dough onto a lightly floured surface; knead lightly. With a floured rolling pin, roll into a 12-inch circle; transfer to the baking sheet, gently pulling the dough back to a 12-inch circle. Slide the crust onto the direct-heat section of the grill. Cover the grill and cook the crust until it is firm and light grill marks are formed, 2–3 minutes.

4. Flip the crust with tongs, then drag to the indirect-heat section of the grill. Sprinkle the cheese over the crust. Top evenly with the peppers and chicken. Return the pizza to the direct-heat section of the grill. Cover the grill and cook until the toppings are hot and the bottom is golden, 3–5 minutes. Grab the edge of the pizza with tongs, then slide onto a board.

Per serving (⅙ of pizza): 325 Cal, 8 g Fat, 2 g Sat Fat, 54 mg Chol, 763 mg Sod, 39 g Carb, 3 g Fib, 23 g Prot, 75 mg Calc. *POINTS: 7.*

Smoked Turkey, Grilled Onion, and Tomato Pizza

Makes 6 servings

Tex-Mex flavors dominate in this simple, smoky pizza—filled with grilled sweet onion and scallions, mesquite-flavored turkey, and melted Swiss cheese.

1 large sweet onion, cut into scant ½-inch-thick slices
1 bunch scallions, trimmed
Cornmeal, for sprinkling
½ recipe (about 1 pound) Basic Pizza Dough— whole-wheat variation (page 11), at room temperature
⅔ cup shredded low-fat Swiss or Gruyère cheese
¼ pound mesquite-flavored sliced smoked turkey breast, chopped
1 cup diced tomato

1. Spray the grill rack with nonstick spray; prepare the grill for indirect cooking (see page 138). Lightly spray the sweet onion and scallions with nonstick spray. Grill the sweet onion slices over direct heat until lightly charred and almost tender, 4–5 minutes on each side. Wrap in foil to steam and help tenderize them, about 10 minutes. Grill the scallions until charred, 2–3 minutes; cut into approximately 1-inch pieces.

2. Lightly sprinkle a large baking sheet with cornmeal. Sprinkle a work surface lightly with flour. Turn the dough onto the surface; knead lightly. With a lightly floured rolling pin, roll into a 12-inch circle. Transfer the circle of dough to the baking sheet, gently pulling the dough back to a 12-inch circle. Slide the crust from the baking sheet onto the direct-heat section of the grill. Cover the grill and cook the crust until it is firm and light grill marks are formed, 2–3 minutes.

3. Flip the crust with tongs, then drag to the indirect-heat section of the grill. Quickly sprinkle ⅓ cup of the cheese over the crust. Top evenly with the onion, scallions, turkey, tomato, and the remaining ⅓ cup cheese, leaving a ½-inch border. Return the pizza to the direct-heat section of the grill. Cover the grill and cook until the toppings are hot and the bottom is golden, 3–5 minutes. Grab the edge of the pizza with tongs, then slide onto a board.

Per serving (⅙ of pizza): 252 Cal, 4 g Fat, 1 g Sat Fat, 12 mg Chol, 622 mg Sod, 42 g Carb, 4 g Fib, 14 g Prot, 133 mg Calc. *POINTS: 5.*

Herbed Duck and Tomato Pizza

Makes 6 servings

Wolfgang Puck, a chef renowned for creating "designer pizzas," is our inspiration in topping this deluxe grilled pizza with duck, goat cheese, fresh herbs, tomatoes, and olives.

2 tablespoons balsamic vinegar

1½ teaspoons packed brown sugar

1 teaspoon minced fresh rosemary leaves

1 large garlic clove, crushed

½ teaspoon salt

1 (¾-pound) skinless boneless duck breast half

1 large red onion, cut crosswise into ¼-inch slices

2 medium plum tomatoes, diced

Cornmeal, for sprinkling

½ recipe (about 1 pound) Basic Pizza Dough (page 10), at room temperature

¼ cup shredded part-skim mozzarella cheese

2 tablespoons lightly packed, thinly sliced basil leaves

½ cup crumbled goat cheese

10 kalamata olives, sliced

1. Combine the vinegar, sugar, rosemary, garlic, and salt in a zip-close plastic bag; transfer 1½ teaspoons of the mixture to a small bowl. Add the duck to the bag. Squeeze out the air and seal the bag; turn to coat the duck. Refrigerate, turning the bag occasionally, 3–4 hours. Cover the reserved marinade and set aside.

2. Spray the grill rack with nonstick spray; prepare the grill for indirect cooking (see page 138). Remove the duck from the bag and grill with the onion over direct heat until the duck is browned with grill marks and the onion is tender, 3–4 minutes on each side (medium-rare for the duck). Wrap the onion in foil; let stand 10 minutes. Cut the duck into thin slices. Toss the tomatoes with the reserved marinade in the small bowl.

3. Lightly sprinkle a large baking sheet with cornmeal. Turn the dough onto a lightly floured surface; knead lightly. With a floured rolling pin, roll into a 12-inch circle; transfer to the baking sheet, gently pulling the dough back to a 12-inch circle. Slide the crust onto the direct-heat section of the grill. Cover the grill and cook the crust until it is firm and light grill marks are formed, 2–3 minutes.

4. Flip the crust with tongs, then drag to the indirect-heat section of the grill. Sprinkle the mozzarella over the crust. Top evenly with the duck and onion, separating the rings. Sprinkle with the basil, tomatoes, goat cheese, and olives. Return the pizza to the direct-heat section of the grill. Cover the grill and cook until the toppings are hot and the bottom is golden, 3–5 minutes. Grab the edge of the pizza with tongs, then slide onto a board.

Per serving (⅙ of pizza): 336 Cal, 10 g Fat, 4 g Sat Fat, 51 mg Chol, 527 mg Sod, 39 g Carb, 2 g Fib, 22 g Prot, 138 mg Calc. *POINTS: 7.*

Grilled Canadian Bacon and Pear Pizza

Makes 6 servings

Pear and smoked ham on whole-wheat bread has been a trendy sandwich in upscale delis and cafés for several years now. This pizza—essentially an open-face grilled sandwich—takes this delicious pairing to new, easy culinary heights.

2 tablespoons fresh lime juice

2 teaspoons honey

2 firm-ripe pears, peeled, halved lengthwise, and cored

2 tablespoons finely diced red onion

1 teaspoon minced fresh thyme

½ pound Canadian bacon slices

Cornmeal, for sprinkling

½ recipe (about 1 pound) Basic Pizza Dough-whole-wheat variation (page 11), at room temperature

⅔ cup reduced-fat Gruyère or Gouda cheese

⅔ cup lightly packed baby spinach leaves

1. Spray the grill rack with nonstick spray; prepare the grill for indirect cooking (see page 138).

2. Combine the lime juice and honey in a medium bowl. Add the pears and toss to coat; remove the pears and set aside. Add the onion and thyme to the lime juice mixture; set aside. Grill the pears and the bacon over direct heat until grill marks appear and the bacon is hot, 1½–2 minutes on each side. Cut the pear into ½-inch dice and slice the bacon into strips.

3. Lightly sprinkle a large baking sheet with cornmeal. Sprinkle a work surface lightly with flour. Turn the dough onto the surface; knead lightly. With a lightly floured rolling pin, roll into a 12-inch circle. Transfer the circle of dough to the baking sheet, gently pulling the dough back to a 12-inch circle. Slide the crust from the baking sheet onto the direct-heat section of the grill. Cover the grill and cook the crust until it is firm and light grill marks are formed, 2–3 minutes.

4. Flip the crust with tongs, then drag to the indirect-heat section of the grill. Quickly sprinkle ⅓ cup of the cheese over the crust. Top evenly with the bacon, spinach, and pears and the remaining ⅓ cup cheese, leaving a ½-inch border. Return the pizza to the direct-heat section of the grill. Cover the grill and cook until the toppings are hot and the bottom is golden, 3–5 minutes. Grab the edge of the pizza with tongs, then slide onto a board.

Per serving (⅙ of pizza): 302 Cal, 6 g Fat, 2 g Sat Fat, 22 mg Chol, 502 mg Sod, 46 g Carb, 4 g Fib, 17 g Prot, 176 mg Calc. *POINTS: 6.*

Chicken, Corn, and Manchego Pizza

Makes 6 servings

Grilled fresh corn on the cob adds color, crunch, and smoky flavor to this pizza.

1 teaspoon ground cumin
½ teaspoon onion powder
¾ teaspoon salt
¼ teaspoon freshly ground pepper
2 (4-ounce) skinless boneless chicken breast halves
2 ears fresh corn, shucked
1 small avocado, pitted and peeled
1 tablespoon fresh lime juice
½ teaspoon green hot pepper sauce (optional)
Cornmeal, for sprinkling
½ recipe (about 1 pound) Basic Pizza Dough—cornmeal variation (page 11), at room temperature
2 ounces manchego cheese, coarsely shredded (½ cup)
3 tablespoons finely chopped fresh cilantro

1. Spray the grill rack with nonstick spray; prepare the grill for indirect cooking (see page 138).
2. Combine the cumin, onion powder, ½ teaspoon of the salt, and the pepper in a cup. Sprinkle onto both sides of the chicken. Grill the chicken over direct heat until just cooked through, about 5 minutes on each side. Grill the corn alongside the chicken, turning as it chars, about 8 minutes. Slice the chicken. Cut the kernels off the cobs.
3. Mash the avocado, lime juice, pepper sauce (if using) and remaining ¼ teaspoon salt in a small bowl.
4. Lightly sprinkle a large baking sheet with cornmeal. Turn the dough onto a lightly floured surface; knead lightly. With a floured rolling pin, roll into a 12-inch circle; transfer to the baking sheet, gently pulling the dough back to a 12-inch circle. Slide the crust onto the direct-heat section of the grill. Cover the grill and cook the crust until it is firm and light grill marks are formed, 2–3 minutes.
5. Flip the crust with tongs, then drag to the indirect-heat section of the grill. Quickly spread the avocado mixture over the crust. Top evenly with the chicken slices, corn, cheese, and cilantro, leaving a ½-inch border. Return the pizza to the direct-heat section of the grill. Cover the grill and cook until the toppings are hot and the bottom is golden, 3–5 minutes. Grab the edge of the pizza with tongs, then slide onto a board.

Per serving (⅙ of pizza): 331 Cal, 10 g Fat, 3 g Sat Fat, 29 mg Chol, 704 mg Sod, 45 g Carb, 4 g Fib, 17 g Prot, 89 mg Calc. *POINTS: 7.*

Chicken, Corn, and
Manchego Pizza

California Sausage, Pepper, and Onion Pizza

Makes 6 servings

Gourmet-flavored chicken or duck sausage, bright yellow bell peppers, and creamy goat cheese make up this strictly California take on sausage-and-pepper pizza.

2 large yellow bell peppers, cut in half lengthwise and seeded

1 large red onion, cut in half lengthwise

2 links (½ pound) low-fat chicken or duck sausage, preferably with Southwestern flavors

1½ teaspoons olive oil

1½ teaspoons white balsamic vinegar

¼ teaspoon salt

Cornmeal, for sprinkling

½ recipe (about 1 pound) Basic Pizza Dough (page 10), at room temperature

½ cup crumbled goat cheese, at room temperature

1. Spray the grill rack with nonstick spray; prepare the grill for indirect cooking (see page 138). Lightly spray the bell peppers and onion with nonstick spray. Grill the bell peppers over direct heat until tender and the skin is charred, 8–10 minutes on each side. Wrap in foil and let stand until cool enough to handle, about 15 minutes. Grill the onion and sausage over direct heat until lightly charred, about 10 minutes, turning as they brown. Peel the peppers and cut into ½-inch strips. Cut the onion into wedges, pull apart and toss with the peppers, oil, vinegar, and salt in a large bowl. Slice the sausage.

2. Lightly sprinkle a large baking sheet with cornmeal. Turn the dough onto a lightly floured surface; knead lightly. With a floured rolling pin, roll into a 12-inch circle; transfer to the baking sheet, gently pulling the dough back to a 12-inch circle. Slide the crust onto the direct-heat section of the grill. Cover the grill and cook the crust until it is firm and light grill marks are formed, 2–3 minutes.

3. Flip the crust with tongs, then drag to the indirect-heat section of the grill. Quickly spread the goat cheese over the crust. Top evenly with the pepper mixture and sausage, leaving a ½-inch border. Return the pizza to the direct-heat section of the grill. Cover the grill and cook until the toppings are hot and the bottom is golden, 3–5 minutes. Grab the edge of the pizza with tongs, then slide onto a board.

Per serving (⅙ of pizza): 292 Cal, 7 g Fat, 3 g Sat Fat, 26 mg Chol, 752 mg Sod, 45 g Carb, 3 g Fib, 13 g Prot, 85 mg Calc. **POINTS: 6.**

 tip The peppers and onion can be grilled ahead of time, combined, and refrigerated, without the dressing, in a zip-close plastic bag for up to three days. Bring to room temperature and toss with the dressing just before topping the pizza.

Grilled Radicchio and Shiitake Pizza

Makes 6 servings

This Italian-inspired combination makes an unusual but delicious pizza. Parrano cheese is imported from Holland and is similar to a creamy Gouda cheese, but sharper.

½ cup fat-free balsamic
   vinaigrette
2 garlic cloves, crushed
1 tablespoon whole-grain
   honey mustard
½ teaspoon chopped
   fresh rosemary
½ teaspoon salt
1½ teaspoons olive oil
⅛ teaspoon freshly ground
   pepper
3 medium plum tomatoes,
   thinly sliced
½ pound fresh shiitake
   mushrooms, stems
   removed
1 large (6-ounce) head
   radicchio lettuce, cut in
   half through the core
Cornmeal, for sprinkling
½ recipe (about 1 pound)
   Basic Pizza Dough—
   semolina variation (page
   11), at room temperature
2 ounces Gruyère or
   paranno cheese,
   shredded (½ cup)

1. Combine the vinaigrette, garlic, mustard, rosemary, and salt in a large bowl; transfer 1½ teaspoons to a large shallow plate. Add the oil and pepper to the plate; mix well. Add the tomatoes, turn to coat, and set aside. Add the mushrooms and radicchio to the remaining vinaigrette mixture in the large bowl; turn to coat and let stand 30 minutes.

2. Spray the grill rack with nonstick spray; prepare the grill for indirect cooking (see page 138). Spray a nonstick vegetable grill basket with nonstick spray; add the mushrooms. Grill over direct heat, turning occasionally, until tender and lightly browned, 8–10 minutes. Place the radicchio alongside the basket directly on the grill and grill until collapsed and browned, 4–5 minutes on each side; transfer the radicchio to a board and slice.

3. Lightly sprinkle a large baking sheet with cornmeal. Turn the dough onto a lightly floured surface; knead lightly. With a floured rolling pin, roll into a 12-inch circle; transfer to the baking sheet, gently pulling the dough back to a 12-inch circle. Slide the crust onto the direct-heat section of the grill. Cover the grill and cook the crust until it is firm and light grill marks are formed, 2–3 minutes.

4. Flip the crust with tongs, then drag to the indirect-heat section of the grill. Sprinkle the cheese over the crust. Top evenly with the mushrooms and radicchio, leaving a ½-inch border. Return the pizza to the direct-heat section of the grill. Cover the grill and cook until the toppings are hot and the bottom is golden, 3–5 minutes. Grab the edge of the pizza with tongs, then slide onto a board. Top the cooked pizza with the marinated tomato slices.

Per serving (⅙ of pizza): 251 Cal, 6 g Fat, 2 g Sat Fat, 9 mg Chol, 425 mg Sod, 41 g Carb, 3 g Fib, 9 g Prot, 108 mg Calc. **POINTS: 5.**

Spicy Sausage and White Bean Pizza

Makes 6 servings

Hot Italian sausage gives a nice kick to this simple pizza, but you can use sweet Italian sausage or any flavored low-fat turkey, chicken, or duck sausage. Be aware that many chicken or duck sausages are fully cooked and only need to be grilled until heated through and grill marks are formed, about 4 minutes on each side.

2 links (½ pound) low-fat hot Italian turkey sausage

4 plum tomatoes, cut in half lengthwise

1 (10-ounce) thin prebaked pizza crust

⅔ cup shredded part-skim mozzarella cheese

1 cup canned cannellini (white kidney) beans, rinsed and drained

1. Spray the grill rack with nonstick spray; prepare the grill. Place the sausage on the grill rack; cover the grill. Grill until cooked through, turning as it browns, about 15 minutes. Lightly spray the tomatoes with nonstick spray, then grill, skin-side down, until the skin is just lightly charred, 2–3 minutes. Transfer the tomatoes to a plate and set aside. Slice the sausage on a slight diagonal; set aside.

2. Place the crust, top-side down, on the grill; cover the grill. Grill until the crust is lightly crisped and golden, 2–3 minutes. Flip the crust with tongs, then sprinkle evenly with ⅓ cup of the cheese. Arrange the sausage and tomatoes on the crust. Scatter the beans on top, then sprinkle with the remaining ⅓ cup cheese. Cover the grill and cook until the toppings are heated through and the crust is deep golden, 2–4 minutes. Grab the edge of the pizza with tongs, then slide onto a board.

Per serving (⅙ of pizza): 262 Cal, 6 g Fat, 2 g Sat Fat, 21 mg Chol, 678 mg Sod, 36 g Carb, 3 g Fib, 16 g Prot, 130 mg Calc. *POINTS: 5.*

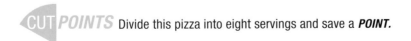

CUT POINTS Divide this pizza into eight servings and save a *POINT.*

Grilled Spanish Tortilla Pizza

Makes 6 servings

Serrano ham, a Spanish ham that's air-dried, often with paprika, is similar to prosciutto. Both are usually served in thin slices and a little packs a lot of flavor. Manchego cheese is the most popular sheep's milk cheese in Spain and, like serrano ham, is full of flavor. The 9- to 10-inch flour tortillas are often referred to as burrito-size tortillas.

2 large red bell peppers, cut in half lengthwise and seeded
1 teaspoon olive oil
⅛ teaspoon saffron threads
1 teaspoon sherry vinegar
1 teaspoon nonpareil capers
3 (9- to 10-inch) whole-wheat or regular flour tortillas
2 ounces manchego cheese, coarsely shredded (½ cup)
2 ounces sliced serrano or prosciutto ham, chopped

1. Spray the grill rack with nonstick spray; prepare the grill. Lightly spray the bell peppers with nonstick spray. Grill until tender and the skin is charred, 8–10 minutes on each side. Wrap in foil and let stand until cool enough to handle, about 15 minutes.

2. Meanwhile, microwave the oil and saffron in a microwavable large bowl on High until very warm, 30–40 seconds. With a fork, whisk in the vinegar and capers. Peel and cut the bell peppers into ½-inch strips. Add the peppers to the saffron vinaigrette and toss together.

3. Place the tortillas on the grill rack. Grill until lightly crisped and golden on the bottom, 1–2 minutes. Flip the tortillas with tongs. Scatter the peppers evenly on the tortillas, then sprinkle with the cheese and ham. Cover the grill and cook until the cheese melts and the bottom is lightly crisped, 1–3 minutes. Cut each tortilla in half crosswise, making a total of 6 pieces.

Per serving (1 piece): 112 Cal, 5 g Fat, 2 g Sat Fat, 14 mg Chol, 341 mg Sod, 11 g Carb, 2 g Fib, 6 g Prot, 78 mg Calc. *POINTS: 2.*

 The peppers can be grilled ahead of time and refrigerated without the dressing in a zip-close plastic bag for up to four days. Bring to room temperature and toss with the dressing before topping the tortillas.

Coastal Pizza

Makes 6 servings

Fresh salmon, scallions, lemon, and thyme make this a pizza fit for any mariner. Try not to overcook the salmon—it will continue to cook a little after removing it from the grill.

3 tablespoons fresh lemon juice

1½ teaspoons minced fresh thyme

¾ teaspoon salt

1 teaspoon extra-virgin olive oil

⅛ teaspoon freshly ground pepper

½ pound center-cut salmon fillet with skin

2 bunches scallions, trimmed

1 cup lightly packed coarsely chopped frisée

Cornmeal, for sprinkling

½ recipe (about 1 pound) Basic Pizza Dough—cornmeal variation (page 11), at room temperature

½ cup crumbled reduced-fat goat cheese

1. Spray the grill rack with nonstick spray; prepare the grill for indirect cooking (see page 138).
2. Combine the lemon juice, thyme, and ½ teaspoon of the salt in a large shallow dish. Transfer 1 tablespoon of the mixture to a medium bowl; add the oil, the remaining ¼ teaspoon salt, and the pepper. Set aside. Add the salmon to the large dish and turn to coat; let stand 15 minutes.
3. Lightly spray the salmon and scallions with nonstick spray. Grill the salmon over direct heat until opaque in the center and lightly charred on the outside, about 4 minutes on each side. Discard the skin. Break the salmon into large flakes. Grill the scallions until lightly charred, 2–3 minutes; cut into approximately 1-inch pieces. Toss the frisée with the reserved dressing in the bowl.
4. Lightly sprinkle a large baking sheet with cornmeal. Turn the dough onto a lightly floured surface; knead lightly. With a floured rolling pin, roll into a 12-inch circle; transfer to the baking sheet, gently pulling the dough back to a 12-inch circle. Slide the crust onto the direct-heat section of the grill. Cover the grill and cook the crust until it is firm and light grill marks are formed, 2–3 minutes.
5. Flip the crust with tongs, then drag to the indirect-heat section of the grill. Quickly spread the cheese over the crust. Top evenly with the frisée, then the salmon and scallions, leaving a ½-inch border. Return the pizza to the direct-heat section of the grill. Cover the grill and cook until the toppings are hot and the bottom is golden, 3–5 minutes. Grab the edge of the pizza with tongs, then slide onto a board.

Per serving (⅙ of pizza): 283 Cal, 6 g Fat, 2 g Sat Fat, 36 mg Chol, 562 mg Sod, 41 g Carb, 4 g Fib, 16 g Prot, 120 mg Calc. *POINTS: 5.*

Coastal Pizza

Shrimp, Hummus, and Red Pepper Pizza

Makes 4 servings

Great for patio parties, this bruschetta-style grilled pizza also makes great appetizers when you cut each serving into quarters. To save time, buy the shrimp already peeled and deveined.

2 medium red bell peppers, cut in half lengthwise and seeded

2 tablespoons thinly sliced fresh basil leaves

½ teaspoon ground cumin

¼ teaspoon salt

¼ teaspoon cayenne (optional)

½ pound large shrimp, peeled and deveined

4 (½-inch-thick) slices Tuscan or peasant bread, 3½ × 6 inches

½ cup 40-spice or regular hummus

1. Spray the grill rack with nonstick spray; prepare the grill. Lightly spray the bell peppers with nonstick spray. Place the peppers on the grill. Grill until tender and the skin is charred, 8–10 minutes on each side. Wrap in foil and let stand until cool enough to handle, about 15 minutes. Peel the peppers, cut into ¼-inch strips, and toss with the basil.

2. Meanwhile, combine the cumin, salt, and cayenne, if using, on a sheet of wax paper. Sprinkle the shrimp with the spices, working over the wax paper. Place the shrimp on the grill rack. Grill until golden on the outside and opaque in the center, 2–3 minutes. Transfer to a cutting board to cool slightly, then chop.

3. Place the bread on the grill rack and grill just until lightly toasted and crisped, about 1 minute on each side. Spread the hummus evenly on one side of each of the toasts. Top with the bell pepper mixture, then the shrimp. Serve at once.

Per serving (1 toast): 195 Cal, 5 g Fat, 1 g Sat Fat, 53 mg Chol, 549 mg Sod, 26 g Carb, 4 g Fib, 12 g Prot, 78 mg Calc. **POINTS: 4.**

 tip To peel and devein shrimp, first remove the shell and tail from the shrimp. Lay the shrimp on a board. Using a sharp paring knife, slice along the back of the shrimp from top to tail, cutting into the shrimp about ⅛ inch. Scrape out the vein with the knife blade and rinse under cold running water.

Lemon-Thyme Zucchini on Flatbread

Makes 6 servings

Flatbreads make quick and delicious alternatives to traditional pizza crusts. Here we use nan—an elongated oval Indian flatbread, similar to a pocketless pita bread. Onion flatbread makes a flavorful alternative to the plain flatbread, if you can find it.

3 tablespoons fresh lemon juice

2–3 garlic cloves, crushed

1½ teaspoons olive oil

1½ teaspoons minced fresh thyme

½ teaspoon salt

2 medium zucchini, cut in half crosswise, then cut into ¼-inch-thick slices, lengthwise

3 (9 × 3½-inch) oval nan flatbreads

½ cup crumbled goat cheese, at room temperature

1. Combine the lemon juice, garlic, oil, thyme, and salt in a zip-close plastic bag; add the zucchini. Squeeze out the air and seal the bag; turn to coat the zucchini. Let stand 30 minutes.

2. Spray the grill rack with nonstick spray; prepare the grill. Remove the zucchini from the plastic bag and place on the grill rack. Grill until tender and grill marks appear, 3–4 minutes on each side. Transfer the zucchini to a plate and set aside.

3. Place the flatbreads on the grill rack and grill until lightly crisped and golden on the bottom, 2–3 minutes. Flip with tongs, then evenly spread the cheese on the flatbreads. Arrange the zucchini on top in slightly overlapping rows and press down lightly. Cover the grill and cook until the bottoms of the flatbreads are lightly crisped, about 3 minutes. Cut each flatbread in half crosswise, making a total of 6 pieces.

Per serving (1 piece): 162 Cal, 4 g Fat, 2 g Sat Fat, 11 mg Chol, 319 mg Sod, 26 g Carb, 2 g Fib, 6 g Prot, 109 mg Calc. *POINTS: 3.*

Grilled Balsamic Eggplant and Feta Pitzas

Makes 6 servings

Eggplant and feta cheese, a traditional Greek pairing, are delicious on grilled pocketless pita breads. Don't skip wrapping the grilled eggplant in foil—the trapped heat creates steam, which helps to tenderize the eggplant.

¼ cup balsamic vinegar

2 large garlic cloves, crushed

1½ teaspoons olive oil

1 teaspoon dried oregano

½ teaspoon salt

¼ teaspoon sugar

1 (1¼-pound) eggplant, cut into 12 rounds

3 (6 to 7-inch) pocketless pita breads

¾ cup crumbled feta cheese

1. Combine the vinegar, garlic, oil, oregano, salt, and sugar in a zip-close plastic bag; add the eggplant. Squeeze out the air and seal the bag; turn to coat the eggplant. Let stand 1 hour.

2. Spray the grill rack with nonstick spray; prepare the grill. Remove the eggplant from the plastic bag and arrange on the grill. Cover the grill and cook the eggplant until tender and charred in spots with grill marks, about 6 minutes on each side. Wrap the eggplant in foil and let stand 15 minutes.

3. Place the pita breads on the grill rack and grill until lightly crisped and golden on the bottom, 2–3 minutes. Flip with tongs, then arrange the eggplant slices evenly on top. Sprinkle evenly with the cheese. Cover the grill and cook until the cheese melts slightly and the breads are lightly crisped, about 3 minutes. Cut each pita in half crosswise, making a total of 6 pieces.

Per serving (1 piece): 148 Cal, 5 g Fat, 3 g Sat Fat, 17 mg Chol, 396 mg Sod, 21 g Carb, 3 g Fib, 6 g Prot, 121 mg Calc. **_POINTS: 3._**

 tip The eggplant can be grilled, allowed to cool completely, then refrigerated in a zip-close plastic bag for up to three days.

Pork and Poblano-Pepper Pizza

Makes 12 servings

Zippy poblano peppers and flavorful cheeses combined with a whole grilled pork tenderloin will yield enough topping for two large or twelve small pizzas here.

3–4 tablespoons fresh
   lime juice
 2 large garlic cloves,
   crushed
 1 teaspoon dried oregano
 1 teaspoon ground cumin
 ½ teaspoon salt
 1 (1 pound) pork tenderloin,
   trimmed of all visible fat
 6 poblano chile peppers
 1 cup crumbled feta cheese
 ½ cup shredded Monterey
   Jack cheese
Cornmeal, for sprinkling
 1 recipe (about 2 pounds)
   Basic Pizza Dough (page
   10), at room temperature
1¼ cups corn, fresh cut from
   the cob or frozen, thawed

1. Combine the lime juice, garlic, oregano, cumin, and salt in a zip-close plastic bag; add the pork. Seal the bag; turn to coat the pork. Refrigerate 1–2 hours.
2. Spray the grill rack with nonstick spray; prepare the grill for indirect cooking (see page 138). Grill the pork over direct heat, turning as it browns, until an instant-read thermometer inserted into the thickest part of the pork registers 160°F for medium, 18–20 minutes. Wrap in foil; let stand 10 minutes, then thinly slice. Meanwhile, grill the peppers over direct heat, turning occasionally, until the skin blisters, about 12 minutes. Wrap in foil and let stand 15 minutes. Peel the peppers, discard the seeds, and cut into thin strips.
3. Combine the feta and Monterey Jack cheeses in a bowl. Sprinkle 2 large baking sheets with cornmeal. Knead the dough on a floured surface; cut in half or 12 pieces. Roll into 2 (12-inch) circles or 12 (4-inch) circles; transfer to the baking sheets, pulling the dough back into shape. Slide the crusts onto the direct-heat section of the grill. Cover the grill and cook until light grill marks form, 2–3 minutes.
4. Flip the crusts with tongs, then drag to the indirect-heat section of the grill. Sprinkle the cheeses over the crusts. Top evenly with the peppers, pork slices, then corn. Return half the pizzas to the direct-heat section of the grill. Cover the grill and cook until the toppings are hot and the bottoms are golden, 4–6 minutes for large pizzas, or 2–3 minutes for individual pizzas, switching the pizzas from the direct-heat of the grill to the indirect-heat section and vice versa once, so they cook evenly.

Per serving (⅙ of large pizza or 1 small pizza): 296 Cal, 7 g Fat, 4 g Sat Fat, 40 mg Chol, 503 mg Sod, 40 g Carb, 2 g Fib, 17 g Prot, 109 mg Calc. **POINTS: 6.**

Pizza Grilling 101

If you've never tried a grilled pizza before, you're in for a pleasant surprise. You'll be hooked the minute you taste one of these crisped and slightly smoky treats. Not only is the eating good, these pies are a lot of fun to make. If you like, enlist a friend or family member to help. Here are a few guidelines for making the perfect grilled pizza:

- To prevent the food or dough from sticking to the grill rack, scrub the rack clean of all debris before you begin, then spray with nonstick spray.

- Prepare the grill for indirect cooking. Here's how: If you have a gas grill, preheat only one side. If you have a charcoal grill, mound the charcoal on one side of the grill. All our grilled pizzas require cooking over the direct-heat section (directly above the heat source) of the grill, but they also require using the indirect section (the unheated side) of the grill while arranging the toppings on the pizzas.

- Have all the toppings and sauces you need to prepare the pizza assembled on a side table before grilling the crust.

- Place the rolled-out pizza dough on a baking sheet (with no rim on at least one side) that has been lightly sprinkled with cornmeal. This will help the dough slide easily off the baking sheet onto the grill.

- If at any time your grilled pizza is browning too quickly, before cooking through, simply drag it to the indirect-cooking section for a minute or two. Tortillas, in particular, are thin, so check the bottoms frequently for overbrowning and move to the cooler section of the grill if necessary.

The Right Tools for the Job

For a successful and calm experience, it's important to set yourself up with everything you'll need before you get started. Here are the essentials:

- A covered grill. If you don't have one, improvise with a lid from a wok, an inverted metal bowl, or a tent of heavy-duty foil.

- Long-handled tongs for dragging the pizza from one section of the grill to the other and to get the pizza off the grill.

- Long oven mitts to protect your hands and forearms.

- A long-handled spatula or spoon for adding the toppings to the cooked pizza crust and to lift one edge of the pizza to check the underside for overbrowning. Use the spatula or spoon to lightly press the toppings onto the crust.

- A grill basket with tightly spaced grids for grilling small topping items that would otherwise fall though the spaces on the grill rack.

- A side table to organize your toppings, sauces, tools, serving plates, and beverage of choice. Once you are this well organized, all you need to concern yourself with is having a good time.

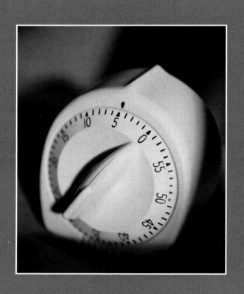

Pizza Pronto

10 Minutes or Less—No Kidding!

Focaccia Stuffed Pizza

Makes 6 servings

Straight from Cannery Row, tuna, marinated mushrooms, roasted peppers, and mozzarella fill this San Francisco-style focaccia. Find freshly baked focaccia breads in an Italian bakery or the bakery section of most large supermarkets.

1 (11-ounce) focaccia, split horizontally

½ cup jarred roasted yellow or red peppers, chopped

½ cup jarred marinated mushrooms, chopped

1 (6-ounce) can solid white tuna packed in water, drained

¾ cup shredded part-skim mozzarella cheese

1. Preheat the broiler. Place the split focaccia on a baking sheet. Broil 4–5 inches from the heat until golden, 30–60 seconds on each side.
2. Toss the peppers, mushrooms, and tuna in a bowl, allowing the tuna to break into bite-size chunks.
3. Top the cut-side of each focaccia half with 1 cup of the tuna mixture, spreading almost to the edge. Sprinkle each piece evenly with the cheese. Broil 4–5 inches from the heat until the cheese melts, 50–70 seconds. Cut each piece of focaccia in half, then sandwich the two halves together, making 2 stuffed focaccia pizzas. Press down lightly for a few seconds to compress, then cut each of the halves into 3 pieces.

Per serving (1 piece): 233 Cal, 8 g Fat, 2 g Sat Fat, 15 mg Chol, 678 mg Sod, 26 g Carb, 1 g Fib, 14 g Prot, 114 mg Calc. **POINTS: 5.**

 tip For an open-face focaccia pizza, cut each of the 2 halves of focaccia into 6 pieces and offer 2 pieces per serving.

Focaccia Stuffed Pizza

Two-Cheese Greek Pizza

Makes 6 servings

Fresh spinach is widely available, but the most convenient and timesaving variety is the microwavable bags of triple-washed baby spinach leaves. Look for them in the bagged-greens area of the produce section of your supermarket. Precrumbled feta also is widely available. If you like, try one of the flavored varieties.

1 (7 to 10-ounce) microwavable bag baby spinach leaves

½ cup marinated artichoke hearts, rinsed, drained, and chopped

1 (10-ounce) thin prebaked pizza crust

½ cup shredded part-skim mozzarella

½ cup crumbled feta cheese

1. Preheat the broiler. Microwave the spinach according to package directions or cook in a large nonstick skillet with 1 tablespoon water, over medium-high heat, until just wilted, about 2 minutes. Coarsely chop the spinach, place in a medium bowl, and stir in the artichokes.

2. Place the pizza crust on a pizza pan or baking sheet. Broil 4–5 inches from the heat until golden, 30–60 seconds on each side.

3. Spread the spinach mixture over the crust to within 1 inch of the edge. Sprinkle the cheeses evenly over the spinach. Broil until the mozzarella melts and the feta partially melts, 50–70 seconds. Cut into 6 wedges.

Per serving (1 wedge): 209 Cal, 8 g Fat, 3 g Sat Fat, 16 mg Chol, 479 mg Sod, 27 g Carb, 3 g Fib, 9 g Prot, 175 mg Calc. **POINTS: 4.**

 tip Instead of plain feta, you might like to try a flavored feta such as sun-dried tomato and basil, or Mediterranean herb.

Hot and Spicy Mexican Tortillizzas

Makes 4 servings

Need a quick fix to please the spicy-food lovers in your house? These chicken and jalapeño-topped tortillas will fill the bill. Preroasted chicken, jarred pickled jalapeños, and a packaged blend of seasoned, shredded Mexican cheeses make it a cinch. If the chicken is very cold, warm it in the microwave for about 20 seconds before using.

1 (8-ounce) bone-in packaged roasted chicken breast, skin and bone removed and coarsely shredded

2 tablespoons pickled jalapeño pepper slices, chopped, + 1 teaspoon liquid from jar

4 teaspoons reduced-fat mayonnaise

1 teaspoon fresh lime juice

1 tablespoon packed fresh cilantro leaves, finely chopped

4 (6-inch) fat-free flour tortillas

½ cup shredded taco cheese (cheddar and Monterey Jack), with seasonings

Lime wedges

1. Combine the chicken, pickled jalapeño pepper and liquid, mayonnaise, lime juice, and cilantro in a medium bowl.

2. Heat a large nonstick skillet over medium heat. Place 2 of the tortillas in the skillet and toast until light golden, about 1 minute on each side. Remove the tortillas and set aside. Repeat with the remaining 2 tortillas.

3. Top each of the tortillas with ¼ cup of the chicken mixture, spreading evenly almost to the edge. Sprinkle each with 2 tablespoons of the cheese. Return to the skillet, 2 tortillas at a time. Cook, covered, over medium-low heat, until the cheese melts and the bottom is crisp and golden, 1–1½ minutes.

Per serving (1 tortillizza): 225 Cal, 8 g Fat, 4 g Sat Fat, 47 mg Chol, 463 mg Sod, 19 g Carb, 1 g Fib, 18 g Prot, 126 mg Calc. *POINTS: 5.*

 tip For even faster results, arrange the tortillas on a baking sheet and broil 4 to 5 inches from the heat until golden, 30 to 60 seconds on each side. Top the tortillas with the chicken mixture, sprinkle with the cheese, then broil another 40 seconds.

Simple Green and White Tortillizzas

Makes 4 servings

Three ingredients give abundant Mexican flavor in these easy pizzas. Serve them with no-*POINT* toppers, such as salsa, shredded lettuce, chopped tomatoes, and thinly sliced scallions. Or judiciously add light sour cream—1½ tablespoons per pizza— for an extra ½ *POINT*.

4 (6-inch) corn tortillas

3 ounces pepperjack cheese, coarsely shredded (¾ cup)

¼ cup packed cilantro leaves, chopped

1. Preheat the broiler. Place the tortillas on a baking sheet. Broil 4–5 inches from the heat until golden, 30–60 seconds on each side.

2. Toss the cheese with the cilantro in a bowl. Sprinkle the cheese mixture evenly over the tortillas. Broil 4–5 inches from the heat until the cheese just begins to melt, 20–40 seconds.

Per serving (1 pizza): 134 Cal, 7 g Fat, 4 g Sat Fat, 20 mg Chol, 174 mg Sod, 12 g Carb, 1 g Fib, 6 g Prot, 198 mg Calc. *POINTS: 3.*

 tip For a mock quesadilla, simply fold each finished tortilla in half.

Caponata and White Bean Pizza

Makes 4 servings

Caponata, an Italian eggplant appetizer, is available in cans or jars in most supermarkets. It is a sweet-sour compote that includes sautéed eggplant, onion, garlic, tomato, herbs, and sometimes green olives. It goes well here on a pizza crust with white beans, spicy hot cherry peppers, and a packaged blend of Italian cheeses to make a snappy meal.

1 (8-ounce) package individual prebaked pizza crusts (two 6-inch crusts), split horizontally to make 4 rounds

1 cup canned small white beans, rinsed and drained

6 tablespoons prepared caponata, chopped

2 tablespoons sliced hot cherry peppers in vinegar, chopped

1 tablespoon vinegar from cherry peppers

1 cup shredded light Italian 4-cheese blend (mozzarella, provolone, Asiago, and Romano)

1. Preheat the broiler. Place the pizza crusts, split-sides up, on a baking sheet. Broil 4–5 inches from the heat until golden, 30–60 seconds on each side.

2. Combine the beans, caponata, cherry peppers, and vinegar in a bowl. Top each of the crusts with a generous ¼ cup of the bean mixture, spreading almost to the edge. Sprinkle each with ¼ cup of the cheese. Broil until the cheese melts, 50–70 seconds.

Per serving (1 round): 341 Cal, 13 g Fat, 5 g Sat Fat, 22 mg Chol, 719 mg Sod, 41 g Carb, 4 g Fib, 15 g Prot, 261 mg Calc. **POINTS: 7.**

 tip Use any leftover caponata for making bruschetta. Simply top a toasted baguette slice with a tablespoon of the caponata.

South-of-the-Border Pizza

Makes 4 servings

Fire-roasted tomatillo salsa adds great smoky flavor to the chicken in this snappy lunch—any green salsa, such as green bell pepper salsa, will do, however. If you have it on hand, substitute 1 cup coarsely shredded leftover chicken or turkey for the roasted chicken.

1 (8-ounce) package individual prebaked pizza crusts (two 6-inch crusts), split horizontally to make 4 rounds

1 (8-ounce) bone-in roasted chicken breast, skin and bone removed and coarsely shredded

6 tablespoons fire-roasted tomatillo salsa

⅓ cup finely diced red bell pepper

1 tablespoon reduced-fat mayonnaise

½ cup shredded reduced-fat Monterey Jack cheese

1. Preheat the broiler. Place the pizza crusts, split-sides up, on a baking sheet. Broil 4–5 inches from the heat until golden, 30–60 seconds on each side.
2. Combine the chicken, salsa, bell pepper, and mayonnaise in a bowl. Top each of the crusts with a generous ¼ cup of the chicken mixture, spreading evenly almost to the edge. Sprinkle each with 2 tablespoons of the cheese. Broil the pizzas until the cheese melts, 50–70 seconds.

Per serving (1 round): 286 Cal, 9 g Fat, 3 g Sat Fat, 40 mg Chol, 458 mg Sod, 30 g Carb, 2 g Fib, 21 g Prot, 128 mg Calc. **_POINTS: 6._**

 tip If you prefer, don't split the crusts horizontally, simply divide the topping between the two crusts, then cut the pizzas in half crosswise. Serve one half pizza per person.

Black Bean Hummus Pitza

Makes 6 servings

Flatbreads (such as pita) and hummus have been eaten together for centuries. Our black bean combination—seasoned with picante sauce, then topped with raw sweet onion and a flavorful cheese blend—has a delicious Mexican taste.

3 pocketless (7-inch) pita breads

1 (15-ounce) can black beans, rinsed and drained

⅓ cup picante sauce or medium salsa

1 tablespoon roasted garlic cloves (4 to 5 cloves)

1 tablespoon reduced-fat mayonnaise

¼ cup very thinly sliced onion

½ cup shredded light Mexican 4-cheese blend (cheddar, Monterey Jack, asadero, and queso blanco)

1. Preheat the broiler. Place the pita breads on a baking sheet. Broil 4–5 inches from the heat until golden, 30–60 seconds on each side.

2. Pulse the beans, picante sauce, garlic, and mayonnaise in a food processor until a chunky paste forms. Top each of the pita breads with a generous ⅓ cup of the bean mixture, spreading almost to the edge. Scatter the onion over the bean mixture, then sprinkle evenly with the cheese. Broil until the cheese melts, 50–70 seconds. Cut each pizza into quarters, making a total of 12 wedges.

Per serving (2 wedges): 216 Cal, 4 g Fat, 2 g Sat Fat, 11 mg Chol, 407 mg Sod, 34 g Carb, 5 g Fib, 10 g Prot, 125 mg Calc. *POINTS: 4.*

tip Look for jarred roasted garlic in the produce section of your supermarket or where prepared garlic is located. This convenience item helps you save time and adds fabulous flavor to the bean mixture. For a pungent garlic taste, substitute roasted garlic-flavored picante sauce for the regular picante sauce and omit the roasted garlic cloves.

San Francisco Roasted
Pepper Bruschetta

San Francisco Roasted Pepper Bruschetta

Makes 6 servings

This lunch-size bruschetta, made on San Francisco's famous sourdough bread, epitomizes the Italian culinary influence of the city on the bay. Fire-roasted red peppers packed in garlic and oil give a lot of flavor, but you can substitute regular roasted red peppers if you prefer.

6 (½-inch-thick) slices sourdough bread, 3½ × 6 inches

¾ cup fire-roasted red peppers in garlic and oil, drained, patted dry, and cut into strips

3 ounces very thinly sliced Genoa salami (8–10 slices), cut into strips

¾ cup shredded light Italian 4-cheese blend (mozzarella, provolone, Asiago, and Romano)

¼ teaspoon dried oregano

1. Preheat the broiler. Arrange the bread on a baking sheet. Broil 4–5 inches from the heat until golden, 30–60 seconds on each side.

2. Arrange the roasted pepper strips evenly on the bread, top with the salami strips, then sprinkle with the cheese and oregano. Broil until the cheese melts, 50–70 seconds.

Per serving (1 bruschetta): 187 Cal, 10 g Fat, 4 g Sat Fat, 22 mg Chol, 582 mg Sod, 15 g Carb, 1 g Fib, 9 g Prot, 124 mg Calc. *POINTS: 4.*

 tip It seems inevitable that toast burns as soon as you turn your back, so watch the bread as it broils, and be sure to arrange your rack to allow 4 to 5 inches between the heat and the top of the bruschetta.

Moroccan Pita Pizzas

Makes 4 servings

Hummus is now available in countless flavors, such as cracked pepper or chili-flavored. Try experimenting with some as an alternative to the scallion variety we've called for here. Look for big, juicy, and flavorful Spanish manzanilla or Sicilian green olives in the pickled vegetable section of your supermarket.

2 pocketless (7-inch) pita breads

6 tablespoons scallion hummus

1 (8-ounce) bone-in roasted chicken breast, skin and bone removed and coarsely shredded

½ cup shredded part-skim mozzarella

6 pitted large imported Spanish manzanilla olives or Sicilian green olives, chopped

1. Preheat the broiler. Place the pita breads on a baking sheet. Broil 4–5 inches from the heat until golden, 30–60 seconds on each side.

2. Spread 3 tablespoons of the hummus evenly onto each of the pita breads, almost to the edge. Top each evenly with the chicken, and sprinkle with the cheese, then the olives. Broil the pizzas until the cheese melts, 50–70 seconds.

Per serving (1 pizza): 269 Cal, 8 g Fat, 3 g Sat Fat, 39 mg Chol, 585 mg Sod, 27 g Carb, 3 g Fib, 22 g Prot, 172 mg Calc. **POINTS: 5.**

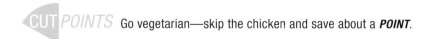 CUT POINTS Go vegetarian—skip the chicken and save about a **POINT**.

Pissaladière Bruschetta

Makes 6 servings

The classic French *pissaladière* toppings of plum tomatoes and anchovies take on an Italian twist in this zesty bruschetta. Look for peasant or Tuscan bread in round loaves and have the baker cut it into thick slices for you. Pick the ripest red tomatoes for best flavor or allow underripe tomatoes to ripen in a closed brown bag until they are bright red but still firm.

6 (½-inch-thick) slices peasant or Tuscan bread, 3½ × 6 inches

4 large plum tomatoes, chopped

1 (2-ounce) can flat anchovy fillets in olive oil, drained and chopped

½ cup very thinly sliced red onion wedges

8 large basil leaves, thinly sliced

4 teaspoons extra-virgin olive oil

1. Preheat the broiler. Place the bread on a baking sheet. Broil 4–5 inches from the heat until golden, 30–60 seconds on each side.

2. Combine the tomatoes, anchovies, onion, and basil in a bowl. Top each bruschetta toast with a generous ½ cup of the tomato mixture, then drizzle each evenly with the oil. Serve at once.

Per serving (1 bruschetta): 130 Cal, 5 g Fat, 1 g Sat Fat, 6 mg Chol, 447 mg Sod, 17 g Carb, 1 g Fib, 5 g Prot, 44 mg Calc. *POINTS: 3.*

Tapenade, Goat Cheese, and Tomato Bruschetta

Makes 4 servings

Tapenade—a delicious olive paste made from kalamata olives finely ground with garlic, herbs, and olive oil—is available already prepared. It can be found in your supermarket, in jars, where imported olives are sold, or in specialty stores. A moist and creamy goat cheese, such as Montrachet from France, works well on these lunch-size toasts.

4 (½-inch-thick) slices peasant or Tuscan bread, 3½ × 5 inches

4 teaspoons prepared tapenade

1 teaspoon extra-virgin olive oil

½ teaspoon balsamic vinegar

¼ teaspoon salt

⅛ teaspoon freshly ground pepper

2 medium ripe tomatoes, cut into 12 thin slices

⅓ cup crumbled goat cheese

1. Preheat the broiler. Place the bread on a baking sheet. Broil 4–5 inches from the heat until golden, 30–60 seconds on each side.

2. Spread each toast evenly with 1 teaspoon of the tapenade.

3. Whisk together the oil, vinegar, salt, and pepper in a pie plate; add the tomatoes and turn to coat. Arrange 3 of the tomato slices, slightly overlapping, on each of the toasts. Sprinkle the tops evenly with the goat cheese. Broil 4–5 inches from the heat until the cheese is softened, 20–40 seconds.

Per serving (1 bruschetta): 124 Cal, 5 g Fat, 2 g Sat Fat, 11 mg Chol, 414 mg Sod, 15 g Carb, 1 g Fib, 4 g Prot, 85 mg Calc. **POINTS: 3.**

 tip Thin tomato slices are best for overlapping. To get thin slices of tomato, use a sharp knife—sometimes a serrated knife works best.

Ham and Mushroom Toasts with Red Pesto

Makes 6 servings

Rosemary-flavored ham is found at the deli counter of most supermarkets. Substitute a peppered ham, if you prefer. Red pesto is made with tomato, basil, garlic, olive oil, and cheese and can be found with bottled condiments or in the Italian specialty section in supermarkets. If you can't find canned wild straw mushrooms in your market, substitute canned sliced button mushrooms.

6 (½-inch-thick) slices rosemary or plain Italian peasant bread, 3½ × 6 inches

1 (15-ounce) can wild straw mushrooms, rinsed and drained

2 ounces sliced lean rosemary ham, cut into strips

2 tablespoons red pesto

¾ cup coarsely shredded fontina cheese

1. Preheat the broiler. Place the bread on a baking sheet. Broil 4–5 inches from the heat until golden, 30–60 seconds on each side.

2. Combine the mushrooms, ham, pesto, and ¼ cup of the cheese in a bowl. Spread ⅓ cup of the mixture on each toast. Sprinkle evenly with the remaining cheese. Broil 4–5 inches from the heat until the cheese melts, 50–70 seconds.

Per serving (1 piece): 184 Cal, 9 g Fat, 4 g Sat Fat, 19 mg Chol, 596 mg Sod, 17 g Carb, 2 g Fib, 9 g Prot, 146 mg Calc. **POINTS: 4.**

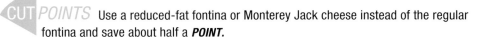 CUT POINTS   Use a reduced-fat fontina or Monterey Jack cheese instead of the regular fontina and save about half a **POINT.**

Deli Fast-Track Reuben Pizza

Makes 4 servings

Reduced-fat products—such as corned beef, Swiss cheese, and Jarlsberg—are available at the deli counter of large supermarkets, and they are perfect for this pizza. Artisan or bakery rye bread refers to premium (not prepackaged) breads. They are crustier and sturdier for this type of moist open-face pizza sandwich.

4 (½-inch-thick) slices artisan or bakery rye bread, 3½ × 5 inches

3 tablespoons light mayonnaise

1 tablespoon ketchup

2 teaspoons sweet pickle relish

1 (8-ounce) can sauerkraut, rinsed and squeezed dry

4 teaspoons whole-grain or dark mustard

8 thin slices (about 3 ounces) reduced-fat corned beef

2 ounces reduced-fat Jarlsberg cheese, coarsely shredded (about ½ cup)

1. Preheat the broiler. Place the bread on a baking sheet. Broil 4–5 inches from the heat until golden, 30-60 seconds on each side.

2. Combine the mayonnaise, ketchup, and relish in a medium bowl; fold in the sauerkraut.

3. Spread 1 teaspoon mustard on each toast; top each with 2 slices of the corned beef. Mound the sauerkraut mixture evenly on the 4 toasts, then sprinkle with the cheese. Broil 4–5 inches from the heat until the cheese melts, 50–70 seconds.

Per serving (1 pizza): 191 Cal, 8 g Fat, 3 g Sat Fat, 22 mg Chol, 1031 mg Sod, 19 g Carb, 3 g Fib, 11 g Prot, 145 mg Calc. **POINTS: 4.**

Artichoke and Tomato Pizza Pronto

Makes 4 servings

Packed with flavor, marinated artichoke hearts go well with plain tomatoes and red onion—just be sure to drain off the oil-based marinade from the artichokes. Toasting the muffins is important to this recipe—it gives a nice crunch and eliminates the possibility of a soggy crust.

4 whole- or honey-wheat English muffins, split

4 small plum tomatoes, chopped

8 pieces (about ½ cup) marinated artichoke hearts, drained and chopped

4 teaspoons finely chopped red onion

¼ teaspoon salt

2 ounces reduced-fat Jarlsberg cheese, coarsely shredded (about ½ cup)

1. Preheat the broiler. Place the muffins, split-side up, on a baking sheet. Broil 4–5 inches from the heat until golden, 50–70 seconds on each side.

2. Combine the tomatoes, artichokes, onion, and salt in a bowl. Top each split side of the muffins with ¼ cup of the tomato mixture and 1 tablespoon cheese. Broil the pizzas until the cheese melts, 50–70 seconds.

Per serving (2 small pizzas): 226 Cal, 6 g Fat, 2 g Sat Fat, 8 mg Chol, 816 mg Sod, 36 g Carb, 7 g Fib, 12 g Prot, 306 mg Calc. *POINTS: 4.*

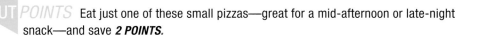

CUT *POINTS*   Eat just one of these small pizzas—great for a mid-afternoon or late-night snack—and save *2 POINTS.*

Avocado, Corn, and Tomato Muffin Pizzas

Makes 4 servings

Charred corn adds a great look as well as good flavor to these quick mini pizzas. Frozen corn—less sweet than canned—works out better for the Southwest flavors here.

1 medium ripe avocado, pitted and peeled

½ lime

¼ teaspoon salt

½ teaspoon hot pepper sauce (optional)

¾ cup frozen corn, thawed and drained

1 medium tomato, coarsely chopped

4 whole-wheat English muffins, split and toasted

2 ounces pepperjack cheese, coarsely shredded (½ cup)

1. Place the avocado in a medium bowl, squeeze the lime half over the top, sprinkle with the salt, and coarsely mash. Add the hot pepper sauce, if using.

2. Preheat the broiler. Heat a large nonstick skillet over high heat. Add the corn and cook until charred in spots, 1–2 minutes. Toss the corn with the tomato in a bowl.

3. Spread 1 tablespoon of the avocado mixture evenly onto the cut side of each toasted muffin half, top with 2 tablespoons of the corn mixture, then sprinkle with 1 tablespoon of the cheese. Broil 4–5 inches from the heat until the cheese melts, 20–40 seconds.

Per serving (2 small pizzas): 287 Cal, 12 g Fat, 4 g Sat Fat, 14 mg Chol, 664 mg Sod, 37 g Carb, 7 g Fib, 11 g Prot, 285 mg Calc. *POINTS: 6.*

CUT *POINTS* If you'd like to save a *POINT*, use four 6-inch fat-free flour tortillas instead of the English muffins, toasting both sides of the tortillas in a dry nonstick skillet until light golden, about 1 minute on each side, and making it one tortilla per serving.

Special Delivery
Mix-and-Match Make-Ahead Toppings

Rosemary-Garlic Pepperonata Topping

Makes 6 servings (2 cups)

Bell peppers are grown throughout southern Italy, including Sicily, and are present in many Italian dishes. These almost-caramelized bell peppers are served as a *primo piatto* (first course) or as a pasta sauce in Italy. Here they make a perfect pizza topping, especially when paired with our fresh semolina pizza dough. For an extra *POINT* per serving, sprinkle the pizza with ½ cup coarsely shredded imported provolone cheese.

1 tablespoon olive oil
3 medium red bell peppers, seeded and cut into thin strips
1 tablespoon nonpareil capers
1 large garlic clove, minced
1½ teaspoons minced fresh rosemary or thyme
1 teaspoon honey
½ teaspoon salt
¼ teaspoon freshly ground pepper

1. Heat a 12-inch nonstick skillet over medium heat. Swirl in the oil, then add the bell peppers. Cook, stirring occasionally, until tender, 15–20 minutes.
2. Add the capers, garlic, rosemary, honey, salt, and pepper. Cook, stirring occasionally, until the peppers are very tender and lightly caramelized, 5–8 minutes.

Per serving (⅓ cup): 35 Cal, 2 g Fat, 0 g Sat Fat, 0 mg Chol, 232 mg Sod, 4 g Carb, 1 g Fib, 0 g Prot, 6 mg Calc. *POINTS: 1.*

To Store the Topping:
Refrigerate in an airtight container for up to four days or freeze for up to two weeks. Let come to room temperature before using.

Use the Topping On:
Half recipe (about 1 pound) Basic Pizza Dough—semolina variation (page 11), rolled into a 12-inch circle. Bake it on a nonstick pizza pan or baking sheet in a 500°F oven, about 8 minutes, then top with the pepper mixture (and provolone cheese, if using) and bake until crisp, 4 to 6 minutes.

Spiced Ricotta and Spinach Topping

Makes 6 servings (2 cups)

Quick and easy, this topping makes good use of incredibly convenient microwavable bags of triple-washed baby spinach leaves. Look for them in the bagged-greens area of the produce section of your supermarket.

1 (7 to 10-ounce) microwavable bag baby spinach leaves

½ cup part-skim ricotta cheese

½ cup shredded part-skim mozzarella cheese

1 large garlic clove, crushed

½ teaspoon salt

¼ teaspoon ground nutmeg

¼ teaspoon freshly ground pepper

1. Cook the spinach according to package directions or in a large skillet with 1 tablespoon water, over medium-high heat, until just wilted, about 1 minute.
2. Combine the spinach, ricotta cheese, mozzarella cheese, garlic, salt, nutmeg, and pepper in a medium bowl.

Per serving (⅓ cup): 63 Cal, 3 g Fat, 2 g Sat Fat, 11 mg Chol, 295 mg Sod, 3 g Carb, 1 g Fib, 6 g Prot, 159 mg Calc. *POINTS: 1.*

To Store the Topping:
Refrigerate in an airtight container for up to 24 hours. Let come to room temperature before using.

Use the Topping On:
Half recipe (about 1 pound) Basic Pizza Dough—semolina variation (page 11), rolled into a 12-inch circle. Bake on a nonstick pizza pan or baking sheet in a 500°F oven, about 8 minutes, then spread with the topping and bake until crisp, 4–6 minutes. For quick pizzas, spread the topping on three large pita breads, split in half and toasted. Bake in a 425°F oven until hot, 6–8 minutes.

Roasted Plum Tomato Topping

Makes 6 servings (2 cups)

Fresh herbs, rather than dried, make all the difference in this rustic Italian classic. Look for nonpareil capers, the smallest variety available—otherwise finely chop the larger capers.

1½ pounds ripe, fresh plum tomatoes, cut in half lengthwise

1 tablespoon extra-virgin olive oil

1 tablespoon nonpareil capers, rinsed and drained

1½ teaspoon salt

2 (5-inch) sprigs fresh rosemary, leaves chopped

8 large basil leaves, thinly sliced

1. Preheat the oven to 450°F. Line a broiler pan with foil; spray the foil with nonstick spray.
2. Arrange the tomatoes, cut-side up, in a single layer on the pan. Roast until tender and lightly charred on the skin side, 20–25 minutes.
3. Toss the tomatoes with the oil, capers, and salt. Stir in the rosemary and basil.

Per serving (⅓ cup): 45 Cal, 3 g Fat, 0 g Sat Fat, 0 mg Chol, 242 mg Sod, 6 g Carb, 1 g Fib, 1 g Prot, 10 mg Calc. **POINTS: 1.**

To Store the Topping:

Omit the rosemary and basil and refrigerate the topping in an airtight container for up to two days. Let the topping come to room temperature, then stir in the rosemary and basil just before using.

Use the Topping On:

Half recipe (about 1 pound) Basic Pizza Dough—semolina variation (page 11), rolled into a 12-inch circle. Bake on a nonstick pizza pan or baking sheet in a 500°F oven, about 8 minutes, then spread with the topping and bake until crisp, 4 to 6 minutes. For quick pizzas, spread the warm topping on six (3½ × 6-inch) slices of toasted peasant bread.

Amatriciana Topping

Makes 6 servings (1⅔ cups)

Amatriciana, a classic bacon-flavored tomato sauce spiked with cream, was created in the Roman town of Amatrice and is commonly served over tube pasta. Here (without the cream), it makes a great pizza topping. For less than a *POINT* extra per serving, sprinkle ½ cup of shredded part-skim mozzarella cheese on top of a six-serving pizza.

4   slices bacon

2   medium onions, cut into very thin wedges (2 cups)

2   large garlic cloves

2   tablespoons dry red wine

¼   teaspoon crushed red pepper

1   (15½-ounce) can fire-roasted or regular crushed tomatoes

8   large basil leaves, thinly sliced

1. Cook the bacon in a nonstick skillet until crisp; drain on paper towels. Reserve 1 tablespoon of the drippings in the skillet. Discard remaining drippings.
2. Add the onions to the skillet and cook over medium heat, stirring, until golden, about 15 minutes. Add the garlic; cook 1 minute. Add the wine and crushed red pepper; cook 1–2 minutes. Stir in the tomatoes; bring to a boil. Reduce the heat and cook until slightly thickened, about 10 minutes. Stir in the basil.

Per serving (scant ⅓ cup): 75 Cal, 4 g Fat, 2 g Sat Fat, 6 mg Chol, 189 mg Sod, 7 g Carb, 1 g Fib, 2 g Prot, 30 mg Calc. *POINTS: 2.*

To Store the Topping:

Omit the basil and store in an airtight container in the refrigerator for up to three days or freeze for up to two weeks. Let the topping come to room temperature or thaw. Stir in the basil just before using.

Use the Topping On:

Half recipe (about 1 pound) Basic Pizza Dough (page 10), rolled into a 12-inch circle. Bake on a nonstick pizza pan or baking sheet in a 500°F oven, about 8 minutes, then spread with the topping and bake until crisp, 4 to 6 minutes. For a quick pizza, spread the topping on a warmed 10-ounce thin prebaked pizza crust and bake in a 425°F oven until hot, 6 to 8 minutes.

Artichoke Pesto Topping

Makes 6 servings (1⅔ cups)

Sun-dried tomatoes packed in oil are moist and flavorful—just be sure to drain off all the oil before using. Look for sun-dried tomatoes in oil that are bright in color. They are usually sweeter in flavor and softer in texture than some varieties that can be almost brown in color.

1 (13.75-ounce) can artichoke hearts, drained

½ cup part-skim ricotta cheese

⅓ cup grated Parmesan cheese

1 tablespoon sun-dried tomato pieces in oil, well drained

1 large garlic clove, chopped

1 teaspoon fresh lemon juice

½ teaspoon salt

⅛ teaspoon cayenne

6 large basil leaves, thinly sliced

Combine the artichoke hearts, ricotta cheese, Parmesan cheese, sun-dried tomatoes, garlic, lemon juice, salt, and cayenne in a food processor; pulse to a chunky paste. Stir in the basil.

Per serving (scant ⅓ cup): 56 Cal, 2 g Fat, 1 g Sat Fat, 6 mg Chol, 366 mg Sod, 7 g Carb, 3 g Fib, 4 g Prot, 80 mg Calc. **POINTS: 1.**

To Store the Topping:

Omit the basil and store in an airtight container in the refrigerator for up to two days. Bring the topping to room temperature, then stir in the basil just before using.

Use the Topping On:

Six toasted small pita breads. Bake in a 425°F oven until hot, 6 to 8 minutes.

Spicy White Bean Topping

Makes 6 servings (1½ cups)

This rich-tasting bean topping, superfast and packed with fiber, will satisfy a big appetite. The hot chili sauce gives it an extra kick—double the amount if you like things truly spicy.

2 teaspoons extra-virgin olive oil
1 large garlic clove
2 tablespoons minced red bell pepper
½ teaspoon Asian hot chile sauce or ⅛ teaspoon cayenne
1 (15½-ounce) can small white beans, rinsed and drained
2 tablespoons low-sodium chicken broth or water

1. Heat a large nonstick skillet over medium heat. Swirl in the oil. Using a garlic press, crush the garlic into the oil. Cook until fragrant, about 10 seconds. Stir in the bell pepper and chile sauce, cook 20 seconds, then remove the skillet from the heat.

2. Remove 1 tablespoon of the beans and mash with the broth in a cup. Stir the whole beans and mashed beans into the bell pepper mixture in the skillet. Cook over medium heat, stirring gently, until heated through.

Per serving (¼ cup): 85 Cal, 2 g Fat, 0 g Sat Fat, 0 mg Chol, 127 mg Sod, 13 g Carb, 3 g Fib, 5 g Prot, 46 mg Calc. *POINTS: 1.*

To Store the Topping:
Refrigerate in an airtight container for up to two days. Bring to room temperature before using.

Use the Topping On:
Six split and toasted English muffins, or three toasted large pita breads cut in half.

Zucchini-Pomodoro Topping

Zucchini-Pomodoro Topping

Makes 6 servings (2½ cups)

This topping can look beautiful on a 12-inch crust, with the tomatoes layered on top of the flat slices of zucchini, but the taste won't be affected if you simply toss the two vegetables together as we have done here.

1 pound ripe, fresh plum
tomatoes, cut in half
lengthwise

1 (5-inch) sprig fresh
rosemary, leaves chopped

½ teaspoon salt

1 tablespoon olive oil

2 small to medium
zucchini, cut crosswise
into ¼-inch slices

2 large garlic cloves

2 (5-inch) sprigs fresh
oregano, leaves chopped

1. Preheat the oven to 450°F. Line a broiler pan with foil; spray the foil with nonstick spray.

2. Arrange the tomatoes, cut-side up, in a single layer on the pan. Roast until tender and lightly charred on the skin side, 20–25 minutes. Sprinkle with the rosemary and ¼ teaspoon of the salt.

3. Meanwhile, heat a large nonstick skillet over medium heat. Swirl in the oil, then add the zucchini in a single layer if possible, or overlapping a bit, if necessary. Cook, turning the zucchini slices as they brown, about 8 minutes. With a garlic press, crush the garlic into the skillet. Cook 1 minute. Sprinkle with the oregano and the remaining ¼ teaspoon salt.

Per serving (generous ⅓ cup): 44 Cal, 3 g Fat, 0 g Sat Fat, 0 mg Chol, 202 mg Sod, 5 g Carb, 1 g Fib, 1 g Prot, 17 mg Calc. **POINTS: 1.**

To Store the Topping:

Place each cooled vegetable in an airtight container in the refrigerator for up to two days. Let come to room temperature before using.

Use the Topping On:

Half recipe (about 1 pound) Basic Pizza Dough (page 10), rolled into a 12-inch circle. Bake on a nonstick pizza pan or baking sheet in a 500°F oven, about 8 minutes, then top with the zucchini and tomatoes and bake until crisp, 4 to 6 minutes. For a quick pizza, layer the zucchini and tomatoes on a warmed 10-ounce thin prebaked pizza crust and bake in a 425°F oven until hot, 6 to 8 minutes.

Shrimp and Black Bean Topping

Makes 6 servings (2½ cups)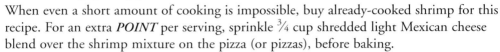

When even a short amount of cooking is impossible, buy already-cooked shrimp for this recipe. For an extra *POINT* per serving, sprinkle ¾ cup shredded light Mexican cheese blend over the shrimp mixture on the pizza (or pizzas), before baking.

¾ **pound cooked shrimp,**
   coarsely chopped
1 **(15½-ounce) can black**
   beans, rinsed and drained
1 **tablespoon extra-virgin**
   olive oil
½ **cup very thin red onion**
   wedges
½ **teaspoon salt**
¼ **teaspoon freshly ground**
   pepper

Combine all the ingredients in a bowl.

Per serving (generous ⅓ cup): 151 Cal, 3 g Fat, 1 g Sat Fat, 111 mg Chol, 439 mg Sod, 14 g Carb, 4 g Fib, 16 g Prot, 59 mg Calc. *POINTS: 2.*

To Store the Topping:
Refrigerate in an airtight container for up to eight hours. Bring to room temperature before using.

Use the Topping On:
Half recipe (about 1 pound) Basic Pizza Dough—cornmeal variation (page 11), rolled into a 12-inch circle. Bake on a nonstick pizza pan or baking sheet in a 500°F oven, about 8 minutes, then top with the shrimp mixture and bake until crisp, 4 to 6 minutes. For quick pizzas, spoon the topping on six pan-toasted 6-inch flour tortillas, then broil 1 minute.

Instant Moroccan Topping

Makes 6 servings (2 cups)

To add flavor, use the oil from the jar of sun-dried tomatoes to sauté the onion. To keep it simple, buy packaged already-crumbled feta cheese.

1 teaspoon of the oil from sun-dried tomatoes

1 medium red onion, diced

1 (13.75-ounce) can artichoke hearts, chopped

¼ cup reduced-fat crumbled feta cheese

10 kalamata olives, pitted and finely chopped

2 teaspoons sun-dried tomato pieces in oil, drained

1 medium garlic clove, minced

¼ teaspoon grated lemon zest

Heat a large nonstick skillet over medium heat. Swirl in the oil, then add the onion. Cook, stirring occasionally, until crisp-tender, about 2 minutes. Remove the skillet from the heat. Add the artichokes, cheese, olives, sun-dried tomato, garlic, and lemon zest; mix well.

Per serving (⅓ cup): 59 Cal, 2 g Fat, 1 g Sat Fat, 6 mg Chol, 274 mg Sod, 8 g Carb, 3 g Fib, 3 g Prot, 64 mg Calc. *POINTS: 1.*

To Store the Topping:
Refrigerate in an airtight container for up to two days. Bring to room temperature before using.

Use the Topping On:
Six (6-inch) pan-toasted corn tortillas. Broil 1 minute.

Caponata Topping

Makes 12 servings (3 cups)

This Italian favorite is great as an appetizer with crackers, as a sauce for pasta, or in this case, for a pizza topping-—there's enough to top two 12-inch pizzas. Or if you prefer, refrigerate half of the caponata, then heat with ½ cup of chicken broth and serve over pasta later in the week.

1 tablespoon olive oil
1 (10-ounce) package fresh white mushrooms
1 medium onion, chopped
1 cup chopped fennel or celery
1 medium eggplant (1-pound), peeled and cut into 1-inch pieces
3 garlic cloves, chopped
2 tablespoons water
1 (14½-ounce) can diced tomatoes
2 tablespoons balsamic vinegar
½ teaspoon sugar
6 pitted green olives, finely chopped
1 tablespoon finely chopped fresh oregano
1 teaspoon salt
¼ teaspoon coarsely ground pepper

1. Heat a 12-inch nonstick skillet over medium-high heat. Swirl in the oil, then add the mushrooms, onion, and fennel. Cook, covered, stirring occasionally, until the liquid is released, 5–7 minutes. Uncover and cook, stirring occasionally, until the vegetables begin to brown, 5–6 minutes.

2. Add the eggplant, garlic, and water. Reduce the heat to medium-low and cook, covered, until the eggplant has softened and reduced, about 12 minutes.

3. Increase the heat to medium-high, and add the tomatoes with their liquid, vinegar, and sugar. Bring to a low boil and cook 10 minutes. Add the olives, oregano, salt, and pepper. Cook until the mixture is very tender, slightly caramelized on the bottom, and no liquid remains, 8–10 minutes.

Per serving (¼ cup): 41 Cal, 2 g Fat, 0 g Sat Fat, 0 mg Chol, 304 mg Sod, 6 g Carb, 2 g Fib, 1 g Prot, 21 mg Calc. ***POINTS: 1.***

To Store the Topping:

Refrigerate in an airtight container for up to five days. Bring to room temperature before using.

Use the Topping On:

One recipe (about 2 pounds) Basic Pizza Dough (page 10), rolled into two (12-inch) circles. Bake on nonstick pizza pans or baking sheets in a 500°F oven, about 8 minutes, then top with the caponata and bake until crisp, 4 to 6 minutes.

Mashed Cauliflower Topping

Makes 12 servings (4 cups)

Sicilian cooking has influenced this unusual pizza topping that pairs so well with our fresh whole-wheat pizza dough. There's enough to top two 12-inch pizzas. Or if you prefer, refrigerate half of the cauliflower, then heat with ½ cup of chicken broth and serve over pasta later in the week. This pizza topping is delicious alone, or for an extra *POINT* per serving, sprinkle each pizza with ½ cup shredded manchego cheese.

1 head cauliflower
(2¼ pounds), cored and
cut into large florets

2 teaspoons of the oil from
sun-dried tomatoes

2 large garlic cloves

1 tablespoon sun-dried
tomato pieces in oil,
drained and minced

½ teaspoon crushed red
pepper (optional)

1 cup low-sodium chicken
broth

1 teaspoon salt

1. Bring a large stockpot two-thirds filled with water to a boil. Add the cauliflower and cook until very tender, 10–13 minutes. Drain, let cool, and chop or break up with fingers into small pieces.

2. Heat a 12-inch nonstick skillet over medium heat. Swirl in the oil, then with a garlic press, crush the garlic into the oil. Add the sun-dried tomatoes and crushed red pepper, if using. Cook, stirring occasionally, until fragrant, about 1 minute. Add the cauliflower, broth, and salt; bring to a boil. Reduce the heat to medium and cook, covered, until the liquid is absorbed and the cauliflower has reduced slightly, 18–20 minutes. Coarsely mash the cauliflower with a potato masher.

Per serving (⅓ cup): 23 Cal, 1 g Fat, 0 g Sat Fat, 0 mg Chol, 214 mg Sod, 3 g Carb, 1 g Fib, 1 g Prot, 13 mg Calc. *POINTS: 0.*

To Store the Topping:

Refrigerate in an airtight container for up to four days. Let come to room temperature before using.

Use the Topping On:

One recipe (about 2 pounds) Basic Pizza Dough– whole-wheat variation (page 11), rolled into two 12-inch circles. Bake on nonstick pizza pans or baking sheets in a 500°F oven, about 8 minutes, then top with the cauliflower (and manchego cheese, if using) and bake until crisp, 4 to 6 minutes.

Double Mushroom Topping

Makes 6 servings (2 cups)

Fresh shiitake mushrooms and prepared marinated mushrooms make for a full-flavored, piquant pizza topping here.

1½ teaspoons olive oil

1 (3.5-ounce) package shiitake mushrooms, stems discarded and caps sliced

2 large garlic cloves, minced

3 large ripe fresh plum tomatoes, diced

1 (12-ounce) jar marinated mushrooms, drained

¼ teaspoon dried thyme

Heat a 12-inch nonstick skillet over medium-high heat. Swirl in the oil, then add the shiitake mushrooms and cook, stirring frequently, until golden, 3–4 minutes. Add the garlic and cook until fragrant, about 30 seconds. Add the tomatoes, marinated mushrooms, and thyme. Cook, stirring occasionally, until the tomatoes soften and thicken slightly, 5–6 minutes.

Per serving (⅓ cup): 34 Cal, 1 g Fat, 0 g Sat Fat, 0 mg Chol, 224 mg Sod, 5 g Carb, 2 g Fib, 2 g Prot, 10 mg Calc. **POINTS: 0.**

To Store the Topping:

Refrigerate in an airtight container for up to two days or freeze for up to two weeks. Let come to room temperature before using.

Use the Topping On:

Twelve (½-ounce) slices toasted Italian bread or six (3½ × 6-inch) slices toasted peasant bread for bruschetta pizzas.

Double Mushroom Topping

Caramelized Onion Topping

Makes 6 servings (1⅓ cups)

Nothing is more delicious than slow-cooked and caramelized sweet onions on a crispy homemade pizza crust—*and* nothing is simpler! If the onions begin to brown during the first 25 minutes, reduce the heat—they should be translucent and tender before the browning begins. If the onions are not browning during the last 20 minutes, increase the heat slightly and cook, stirring occasionally, until they caramelize. This pizza topping is delicious alone, or for an extra *POINT* per serving, sprinkle the pizza with ½ cup shredded mozzarella or crumbled goat cheese.

1 large sweet onion
1 tablespoon olive oil
1 tablespoon minced fresh
   herbs, such as oregano,
   thyme, or rosemary
1 teaspoon salt

1. Cut the onion in half lengthwise, then cut into very thin wedges.

2. Heat a 12-inch nonstick skillet over medium-low heat. Swirl in the oil, then add the onion and cook, stirring occasionally, until translucent and tender, 20–25 minutes.

3. Increase the heat to medium, then sprinkle the onions with the herbs and salt. Cook, stirring occasionally, until golden, caramelized, and reduced to about 1⅓ cups, 15–20 minutes.

Per serving (scant ¼ cup): 30 Cal, 2 g Fat, 0 g Sat Fat, 0 mg Chol, 388 mg Sod, 2 g Carb, 1 g Fib, 0 g Prot, 42 mg Calc. *POINTS: 1.*

To Store the Topping:
Refrigerate in an airtight container for up to three days. Let come to room temperature before using.

Use the Topping On:
Half recipe (about 1 pound) Basic Pizza Dough (page 10), rolled into a 12-inch circle. Bake it on a nonstick pizza pan or baking sheet in a 500°F oven, about 8 minutes, then top with the onion (and mozzarella or goat cheese, if using) and bake until crisp, 4 to 6 minutes. For a quick pizza, place the onions (and cheese, if using) on a warmed 10-ounce thin prebaked pizza crust and bake in a 425°F oven until hot, 6 to 8 minutes.

Roasted Vegetable Sauce Topping

Makes 4 servings (1¼ cups)

This incredible sauce is really a chunky puree of delicious healthy vegetables. For an extra *POINT* per serving, sprinkle each individual pizza with 1½ tablespoons of coarsely shredded cheddar cheese.

½ (10-ounce) package button mushrooms (about 2 cups)

1 medium red bell pepper, seeded and quartered

1 medium onion, quartered

¾ teaspoon salt

2 medium tomatoes, cut into thick slices

2 teaspoons olive oil

1 large garlic clove, sliced

¼ teaspoon freshly ground pepper

1. Preheat the oven to 450°F. Spray a broiler pan with nonstick spray.
2. Place the mushrooms, bell pepper, and onion on the pan in a single layer; sprinkle with ¼ teaspoon of the salt. Cover the pan with foil and bake until the vegetables release their liquid, 10 minutes. Uncover, then add the tomatoes, being sure the slices are flat on the pan. Spray lightly with nonstick spray. Bake until the vegetables are all tender and caramelized, about 20 minutes.
3. Microwave the oil and garlic in a microwavable cup just until fragrant, about 30 seconds.
4. Transfer the vegetables to a blender. Add the oil-garlic mixture, the remaining ½ teaspoon salt, and the pepper. Add 1 tablespoon water to the broiler pan and scrape the drippings with a rubber spatula into the blender. Blend the mixture to a chunky puree, scraping the sides of the blender as necessary.

Per serving (generous ¼ cup): 59 Cal, 3 g Fat, 0 g Sat Fat, 0 mg Chol, 444 mg Sod, 8 g Carb, 2 g Fib, 2 g Prot, 14 mg Calc. *POINTS: 1.*

To Store the Topping:
Refrigerate in an airtight container for up to two days. Let come to room temperature before using.

Use the Topping On:
Four (6-inch) pan-toasted flour tortillas or four (3½ × 6-inch) slices toasted peasant bread (add cheddar cheese, if using) and broil 1 minute.

Winter Tomato Compote Topping

Makes 6 servings (1½ cups)

Cherry tomatoes made into tomato sauce? It may sound strange, but in winter they're a great fresh tomato alternative for making sauce when good ripe tomatoes are hard to find.

1 tablespoon olive oil
⅓ cup finely chopped
   shallot
1 pint cherry tomatoes
1½ teaspoons balsamic
   vinegar
1 teaspoon chopped fresh
   oregano, or ½ teaspoon
   dried
½ teaspoon salt
½ teaspoon crushed red
   pepper (optional)

Heat a large nonstick skillet over medium heat. Swirl in the oil, then add the shallot. Cook, stirring occasionally, until translucent, about 1 minute. Add the tomatoes and cook 1 minute. Stir in the vinegar, oregano, salt, and crushed red pepper (if using). Cook until the tomatoes soften but do not totally lose their shape, 1–1½ minutes.

Per serving (¼ cup): 36 Cal, 2 g Fat, 0 g Sat Fat, 0 mg Chol, 201 mg Sod, 4 g Carb, 1 g Fib, 1 g Prot, 11 mg Calc. *POINTS: 1.*

To Store the Topping:
Refrigerate in an airtight container for up to one day. Let come to room temperature before using.

Use the Topping On:
Half recipe (about 1 pound) Basic Pizza Dough (page 10), rolled into a 12-inch circle. Bake it on a nonstick pizza pan or baking sheet in a 500°F oven, about 8 minutes, then top with the compote and bake until crisp, 4 to 6 minutes. For quick pizzas, spoon the warm topping on six (3½ × 6-inch) slices toasted peasant bread.

Create Your Own Pizza

There's nothing like the fun of concocting your own pizza. This chapter gives 15 make-ahead pizza toppings, which you can mix and match with a favorite base or crust. At the end of each topping recipe, we suggest bases to go with that topping and give directions for assembling the pizza, but you can put together your own favorite combinations, according to your fancy and the time you have to spend. You can make the topping on the weekend, store it according to our recipe directions, then use it during the week for a quick meal on one of the following bases, adding the appropriate number of *POINTS*.

- 1 serving Basic Pizza Dough (page 10): *3 POINTS*
- 1 serving cornmeal or whole-wheat variation of Basic Pizza Dough (page 11): *3 POINTS*
- 1 serving semolina variation of Basic Pizza Dough (page 11): *4 POINTS*
- 1 serving store-bought refrigerated pizza dough (one-sixth of dough): *5 POINTS*
- 1 serving thin prebaked pizza crust (one-sixth of crust): *4 POINTS*
- 1 ($3\frac{1}{2}$ × 6-inch) slice peasant bread: *3 POINTS*
- 1 (6-inch) corn tortilla: *2 POINTS*
- 1 (6-inch) flour tortilla: *2 POINTS*
- 1 large white or whole-wheat pita bread: *2 POINTS*
- 1 small white or whole-wheat pita bread: *1 POINT*
- 1 English muffin: *2 POINTS*
- 1 ($\frac{1}{2}$-ounce) slice Italian or French bread: *1 POINT*

Pizza Sidekicks

Salads and Sides to Pair with Your Pie

Antipasto Salad

Makes 6 servings

An everyday lettuce-and-tomato salad is raised to new culinary heights with flavorful prosciutto and provolone and a zesty dressing. This salad makes a perfect beginning or accompaniment to most of our Italian-inspired pizzas.

1 tablespoon extra-virgin olive oil

1 tablespoon fresh lemon juice

1 tablespoon capers, rinsed and drained

1 small garlic clove, minced

½ teaspoon dried oregano

¼ teaspoon freshly ground pepper

1 cup cooked elbow macaroni or other small pasta

1 small cucumber, peeled, seeded, and diced (about 1 cup)

1 large ripe tomato, diced

1 small red onion, diced

4 cups shredded romaine lettuce

1 ounce thinly sliced prosciutto, cut into thin strips

1 ounce sliced provolone cheese, cut into thin strips

1. Combine the oil, lemon juice, capers, garlic, oregano, and pepper in a large bowl. Add the macaroni, cucumber, tomato, and onion; toss well to coat.

2. Add the lettuce, prosciutto, and cheese; toss lightly and serve at once.

Per serving (scant 1 cup): 102 Cal, 5 g Fat, 1 g Sat Fat, 8 mg Chol, 241 mg Sod, 11 g Carb, 2 g Fib, 5 g Prot, 57 mg Calc. **POINTS: 2.**

 tip For extraordinary flavor, use prosciutto imported from Italy, such as prosciutto di Parma, and aged provolone cheese, thinly sliced or shaved at the last minute.

Mixed Greens with Tomato-Basil Dressing

Makes 6 servings

Summer's jewels—beefsteak tomatoes—are the key to making the zesty dressing that is the star of this salad. But don't be fooled into thinking this is a summertime only recipe—anytime you have ripe red tomatoes or cherry or grape tomatoes and fresh basil on hand, you can make this tasty topper. For a change of pace, substitute romaine lettuce, arugula, or Belgian endive leaves for the mesclun.

1 beefsteak tomato, cut into wedges
½ small red onion, cut into wedges
1 garlic clove, cut in half
2 tablespoons balsamic vinegar
½ teaspoon salt
½ teaspoon sugar
⅛ teaspoon freshly ground pepper
5–6 fresh basil leaves
12 cups mesclun salad greens
2 tablespoons freshly grated Parmesan cheese

1. Puree the tomato, onion, garlic, vinegar, salt, sugar, pepper, and basil in a food processor or blender.
2. Divide the greens among 6 salad plates. Spoon about 3 tablespoons of the dressing over each serving. Sprinkle evenly with the cheese.

Per serving (2 cups greens with 3 tablespoons dressing): 41 Cal, 1 g Fat, 1 g Sat Fat, 2 mg Chol, 265 mg Sod, 6 g Carb, 3 g Fib, 3 g Prot, 94 mg Calc. **POINTS: 0.**

tip Pair this refreshing salad with Roasted Onion and Olive Pizza with Goat Cheese, (page 99).

Warm Spinach and Radish Salad with Bacon

Makes 6 servings 🕐

Hot bacon dressing drizzled over fresh spinach leaves (to slightly wilt them) is an all-time favorite. We crisp the flavorful bacon, discard the fat, and add a few radish slices for color, texture, and snappy flavor.

3 **thick-cut bacon slices, diced**

4 **teaspoons olive oil**

1 **medium red onion, finely chopped**

¼ **cup white balsamic vinegar**

¼ **teaspoon salt**

¼ **teaspoon freshly ground pepper**

1 **(10-ounce) bag fresh triple-washed spinach, torn**

1 **bunch radishes, trimmed and thinly sliced**

1. Heat a large nonstick skillet over medium heat. Add the bacon and cook, stirring occasionally, until crisp and browned, about 5 minutes. With a slotted spoon, lift the bacon onto paper towels; set aside. Pour the fat from the skillet and discard.

2. Swirl the oil into the same skillet. Add the onion and cook, stirring occasionally, until softened, about 5 minutes. Stir in the vinegar, salt, and pepper; heat for 30 seconds.

3. Place the spinach and radishes in a salad bowl. Add the hot dressing and toss to coat. Sprinkle with the bacon and serve at once.

Per serving (1⅓ cups): 78 Cal, 5 g Fat, 1 g Sat Fat, 5 mg Chol, 267 mg Sod, 5 g Carb, 1 g Fib, 3 g Prot, 57 mg Calc. *POINTS: 2.*

 tip White balsamic vinegar, slightly sweeter than the dark and a touch less intense, is perfect in this salad. Find it in large supermarkets and specialty stores. Try this mellow salad with Spicy Pork Taco Pizzas (page 43).

Belgian Endive with Pear and Cilantro Topping

Makes 4 servings

Fresh ripe pear adds a welcome sweetness to the tangy topping of this salad. Prepare the dressing *before* you peel and dice the pear, then cut the pear and add to the dressing as soon as you cut it, to prevent it from turning brown from exposure to the air.

2 tablespoons red-wine vinegar

2 tablespoons chopped fresh cilantro

1 tablespoon olive oil

1 tablespoon minced shallot

½ teaspoon sugar

½ teaspoon Dijon mustard

¼ teaspoon salt

⅛ teaspoon freshly ground pepper

1 ripe pear, peeled and diced

2 large heads Belgian endive

1. Combine the vinegar, cilantro, oil, shallot, sugar, mustard, salt, and pepper in a medium bowl. Add the pear and toss gently to coat.
2. Separate 12 outer leaves from the heads of endive. Chop the remaining endive and mix with the pear and dressing. Arrange the endive leaves on 4 plates. Spoon the pear mixture over the endive leaves and serve at once.

Per serving (3 endive leaves with ½ cup topping): 63 Cal, 4 g Fat, 1 g Sat Fat, 0 mg Chol, 167 mg Sod, 9 g Carb, 2 g Fib, 1 g Prot, 18 mg Calc. ***POINTS: 1.***

 tip To fully appreciate this elegant salad, serve it separately, as an hors d'oeuvre, at the table. It makes a perfect prelude to Lobster, Goat Cheese, and Sun-Dried Tomato Pizza (page 59).

Avocado, Grapefruit, and Apple with Poppy Seed Dressing

Avocado, Grapefruit, and Apple with Poppy Seed Dressing

Makes 6 servings

Creamy avocados add rich flavor to this salad. When buying avocados, choose a fruit that yields to the touch. You can speed up the ripening process by putting an avocado in a brown paper bag with a slice of bread. Mexican Pizza Grande (page 98) makes a wonderful match for this creamy, fruity salad.

1 large grapefruit

2 tablespoons fat-free mayonnaise

2 teaspoons fresh lime juice

½ teaspoon sugar

½ teaspoon poppy seeds

¼ teaspoon salt

1 small ripe avocado

1 red apple, thinly sliced

12 Boston lettuce leaves

1 tablespoon coarsely chopped toasted pecans

1. Cut away the peel and all the yellow pith from the grapefruit. Hold the grapefruit over a bowl, then cut away the sections from the membranes, letting sections and juice fall into the bowl. Transfer 2 table-spoons of the juices to a medium bowl.

2. Add the mayonnaise, lime juice, sugar, poppy seeds, and salt to the grapefruit juice; mix well. With a slotted spoon remove the grapefruit from the remaining juice and add to the mayonnaise mixture (reserve the remaining grapefruit juice for another use).

3. Peel and slice the avocado. Add the avocado and apple to the mayonnaise mixture; toss to coat.

4. Arrange the lettuce on 6 plates. Spoon the salad (about ½ cup) onto each plate. Sprinkle with the pecans and serve at once.

Per serving (2 lettuce leaves with ½ cup salad): 83 Cal, 4 g Fat, 1 g Sat Fat, 0 mg Chol, 133 mg Sod, 12 g Carb, 3 g Fib, 1 g Prot, 18 mg Calc. *POINTS: 1.*

 tip To toast pecans, place them in a small dry skillet over medium-low heat. Cook, shaking the pan and stirring constantly, until lightly browned and fragrant, 3 to 4 minutes. Watch them carefully when toasting; pecans can burn quickly. Transfer the pecans to a plate to cool.

Minted Slaw with Orange and Cranberries

Makes 8 servings

With a refreshing orange-mint dressing, this slaw serves as a crunchy foil to many of our cheese pizzas. If fresh mint is not available, avoid dried mint—flavorwise, it just doesn't cut it. Chopped parsley is a suitable substitute for the mint.

1 navel orange, peeled and cut into sections, 1 tablespoon juice reserved

2 tablespoons cider vinegar

1 tablespoon sunflower oil

1 teaspoon sugar

¼ teaspoon salt

¼ teaspoon freshly ground pepper

1 small green Savoy cabbage, shredded

1 small red onion, halved lengthwise, then very thinly sliced crosswise

⅓ cup chopped fresh mint

⅓ cup dried cranberries

1. Combine the orange juice, vinegar, oil, sugar, salt, and pepper in a small bowl.

2. Combine the cabbage, orange sections, onion, mint, and cranberries in a large bowl. Add the dressing; toss well to coat. Let stand about 10 minutes so the flavors can blend.

Per serving (¾ cup): 58 Cal, 2 g Fat, 0 g Sat Fat, 0 mg Chol, 89 mg Sod, 10 g Carb, 3 g Fib, 1 g Prot, 35 mg Calc. *POINTS: 1.*

 tip Unlike most salads, leftovers of this zippy slaw keep well in the refrigerator for up to two days.

Jicama and Tomato Salad

Makes 4 servings

This crunchy sweet-and-sour Mexican salad makes a refreshing side to any of our south-of-the-border pizzas. Find jicama in the produce section of most supermarkets or in Latin markets. For a creamy counterpoint (and an extra *POINT* per serving), stir in ½ cup diced avocado just before serving.

1 small (about 10-ounce) jicama, peeled and shredded (about 2 cups)

2 plum tomatoes, chopped

½ cup finely chopped red onion

1 tablespoon chopped fresh cilantro or parsley

4 teaspoons fresh lime juice

1 tablespoon canola oil

¼ teaspoon salt

¼ teaspoon sugar

⅛ teaspoon crushed red pepper

Combine the jicama, tomatoes, onion, and cilantro in a medium bowl. Add the lime juice, oil, salt, sugar, and crushed red pepper; toss well to coat. Serve at once or cover and refrigerate for up to 2 days.

Per serving (generous ½ cup): 72 Cal, 4 g Fat, 0 g Sat Fat, 0 mg Chol, 152 mg Sod, 10 g Carb, 4 g Fib, 1 g Prot, 14 mg Calc. *POINTS: 1.*

 tip Use a vegetable peeler to remove the tough outer skin of the jicama. For a pretty presentation, nestle the salad in a Boston lettuce cup.

Beet and Fennel Salad with Chive Vinaigrette

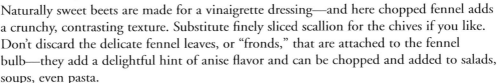

Makes 4 servings

Naturally sweet beets are made for a vinaigrette dressing—and here chopped fennel adds a crunchy, contrasting texture. Substitute finely sliced scallion for the chives if you like. Don't discard the delicate fennel leaves, or "fronds," that are attached to the fennel bulb—they add a delightful hint of anise flavor and can be chopped and added to salads, soups, even pasta.

1 **pound fresh beets, peeled**
3 **tablespoons rice-wine vinegar**
1 **tablespoon canola oil**
½ **teaspoon salt**
½ **teaspoon sugar**
2 **tablespoons snipped fresh chives**
½ **small fennel bulb, chopped (1 cup)**
2 **tablespoons chopped fennel leaves or parsley**

1. Bring the beets, with enough water to cover, to a boil in a saucepan. Reduce the heat and simmer, partially covered, until tender, about 35 minutes. Drain and let stand until cool enough to handle. Cut into ½-inch dice; place in a medium bowl.

2. Combine the vinegar, oil, salt, and sugar in a small bowl; stir in the chives. Pour the mixture over the warm beets; toss to coat. Stir in the fennel and fennel leaves. Serve at once while slightly warm, or at room temperature. Or cover and refrigerate for up to 2 days and serve chilled.

Per serving (¾ cup): 86 Cal, 4 g Fat, 0 g Sat Fat, 0 mg Chol, 384 mg Sod, 13 g Carb, 3 g Fib, 2 g Prot, 31 mg Calc. **POINTS: 1.**

tip You can team this salad with Tuna Niçoise on Potato-Rosemary Pizza (page 58).

Chunky Tomato, Cucumber, and Mozzarella Salad

Makes 4 servings

Gather summer's bounty of tomatoes, cucumbers, and fresh basil. Add a really good balsamic vinegar and assemble this simple treat. Choose an authentic balsamic vinegar from Modena, Italy, for intense, complex flavor (and thank Luciano Pavarotti, a Modena native who sang the praises of balsamic 20 years ago, for encouraging the balsamic craze in this country). To avoid bruising the basil, gently stir it in last, or if you prefer, substitute 2 tablespoons chopped parsley for the basil.

 2 ripe medium tomatoes,
   cut into ½-inch chunks
 1 cucumber, peeled,
   seeded, and cut into
   ½-inch chunks
 2 ounces part-skim
   mozzarella cheese, diced
 2 tablespoons finely
   chopped red onion
1½ tablespoons balsamic
   vinegar
 1 teaspoon extra-virgin
   olive oil
 ¼ teaspoon salt
 ¼ teaspoon sugar
Freshly ground pepper,
   to taste
10 large basil leaves,
   cut into thin strips

Combine the tomatoes, cucumber, mozzarella, onion, vinegar, oil, salt, sugar, and pepper in a medium bowl. Gently stir in the basil. Serve at once.

Per serving (¾ cup): 76 Cal, 4 g Fat, 2 g Sat Fat, 8 mg Chol, 228 mg Sod, 6 g Carb, 1 g Fib, 5 g Prot, 119 mg Calc. ***POINTS: 2.***

 Fresh basil or lettuce cut into thin strips is referred to as a *chiffonade*. An easy way to make a basil *chiffonade* is to stack the whole basil leaves on top of one another, roll them up from one long end, then cut the roll into thin slices. Ample cheese in this salad makes it a good match for our Pizza Margherita with Roasted Grape Tomatoes (page 82).

Tomato and Orange Stacks

Makes 4 servings

Be sure to choose ripe tomatoes the same size as the peeled oranges to make evenly balanced stacks. If you like, substitute yellow tomatoes for the red and place the stacks on a red or green lettuce leaf.

2 navel oranges
2 ripe tomatoes
2 tablespoons balsamic vinegar
2 tablespoons chopped parsley
1 tablespoon orange juice
2 teaspoons olive oil
¼ teaspoon salt
⅛ teaspoon freshly ground pepper

1. Grate 1 teaspoon orange zest from one of the oranges; place in a small bowl and set aside.
2. Cut away the peel from both of the oranges, removing all of the yellow pith. Trim off ¼ inch from the ends of each orange, then cut each orange into 4 crosswise slices.
3. Trim off ¼ inch from the ends of each tomato, then cut each tomato into 4 crosswise slices.
4. Add the vinegar, parsley, orange juice, oil, salt, and pepper to the orange zest; mix well.
5. Stack 2 tomato and 2 orange slices alternately on each of 4 salad plates. Drizzle each stack with about 1 tablespoon of the dressing. Serve at once.

Per serving (1 stack): 79 Cal, 3 g Fat, 0 g Sat Fat, 0 mg Chol, 157 mg Sod, 14 g Carb, 3 g Fib, 2 g Prot, 38 mg Calc. *POINTS: 1.*

 Don't refrigerate this salad or the tomatoes before assembling—cold damages the flavor and texture of tomatoes. If you like you can use chilled oranges. Serve this salad as a dramatic first course to any of our Deluxe Pizzas.

Tomato and Orange Stacks

Mixed Vegetable Pickles

Makes 24 servings

Vegetables preserved in a vinegar-sugar mixture has been popular for years, long before refrigeration was available. Today, if you don't want to fuss with sterilizing and preserving these vegetables, you can simply store them in glass jars in the refrigerator for up to 1 month.

2 cups cider vinegar

1 cup water

¾ cup sugar

2 tablespoons mustard seeds

2 teaspoons turmeric

1 teaspoon salt

½ teaspoon crushed red pepper

1 (1-pound) bag baby carrots

1 small cauliflower, cut into small florets (about 6 cups)

½ pound fresh green beans, trimmed and cut in half

4 ears fresh corn, husked and kernels removed (about 2 cups)

1 onion, chopped

1. Bring the vinegar, water, sugar, mustard seeds, turmeric, salt, and crushed red pepper to a boil in a Dutch oven. Add the carrots; return to a boil. Reduce the heat and simmer, covered, about 5 minutes.

2. Add the cauliflower, green beans, corn, and onion; return to a boil. Reduce the heat and simmer, covered, until the vegetables are crisp-tender, about 8 minutes.

3. Pack the hot mixture into hot, sterilized ball jars, leaving ⅛ inch head space. Seal with caps and screw lids. Immerse the jars into a deep kettle with enough boiling water to come 1 inch above the jars. Cover and simmer 15 minutes. Carefully lift the jars from the water and let cool completely. Store in a cool, dark place for up to 6 months.

Per serving (⅓ cup): 62 Cal, 1 g Fat, 0 g Sat Fat, 0 mg Chol, 114 mg Sod, 14 g Carb, 2 g Fib, 2 g Prot, 22 mg Calc. **POINTS: 1.**

 tip While peeled baby carrots win kudos for convenience, they can be lacking in flavor. Look for unpeeled organic varieties, which will have a better taste. Keep these pickles on hand as a convenient go-along for any of our pizzas.

Grilled Summer Vegetables with Fresh Salsa

Makes 4 servings

If you're planning on lighting the grill for one of our grilled pizzas, grill these vegetables first, then allow them to come to room temperature while the pizza cooks. Either reheat them on the grill for 1 to 2 minutes or serve them at room temperature. You can make the salsa up to three days ahead and keep it in the refrigerator.

1 cup grape tomatoes

½ small red onion

2 tablespoons fresh cilantro leaves

2 teaspoons fresh lemon juice

¾ teaspoon salt

¼ teaspoon ground cumin

⅛ teaspoon cayenne

3 baby Italian eggplants, each cut into 4 lengthwise slices

2 medium zucchini, each cut into 4 lengthwise slices

1 yellow squash, cut into 4 lengthwise slices

1. To make the salsa, combine the tomatoes, onion, cilantro, juice, ¼ teaspoon of the salt, the cumin, and cayenne in a food processor; pulse until coarsely chopped. Transfer to a small bowl and set aside about 15 minutes to let the flavors develop.

2. Spray the grill rack with nonstick spray. Prepare the grill. Lightly spray the eggplant, zucchini, and squash with nonstick spray. Arrange on the rack. Sprinkle with the remaining ½ teaspoon salt. Grill, turning occasionally, until lightly charred and softened, about 10 minutes. Serve with the salsa.

Per serving (¼ of vegetables with 3 tablespoons salsa): 87 Cal, 1 g Fat, 0 g Sat Fat, 0 mg Chol, 445 mg Sod, 19 g Carb, 7 g Fib, 4 g Prot, 39 mg Calc. *POINTS: 1.*

Primavera Sauté

Makes 6 servings

We allow the flavors from these fresh spring vegetables to shine by adding just a sprinkling of lemon, salt, and pepper. Garnish the dish with thin strips of lemon zest or serve with a few fresh shavings of Parmesan cheese. An added bonus: It's good hot or cold!

2 teaspoons olive oil

1 bunch scallions, sliced on the diagonal (whites and 2 inches of green portion only)

1 bunch fresh asparagus, trimmed and cut into diagonal 1-inch pieces

1 bunch watercress, cleaned and coarsely chopped

2 teaspoons fresh lemon juice

½ teaspoon salt

Freshly ground pepper, to taste

1. Heat a large nonstick skillet over medium-high heat. Swirl in the oil, then add the scallions and asparagus. Cook, stirring occasionally, until crisp-tender, about 5 minutes.

2. Stir in the watercress, lemon juice, salt, and pepper. Cook, stirring occasionally, until the watercress just begins to wilt, about 2 minutes. Serve at once. Or cover and refrigerate for up to 2 days and serve chilled.

Per serving (½ cup): 29 Cal, 2 g Fat, 0 g Sat Fat, 0 mg Chol, 213 mg Sod, 3 g Carb, 1 g Fib, 2 g Prot, 55 mg Calc. ***POINTS: 1.***

 tip You can round out the Anchovy, Onion, and Olive Pizza (page 64) with this fresh green-vegetable sauté.

Steamed Fall Vegetables with Garlic

Makes 6 servings

Favorite fall vegetables such as broccoli, cauliflower, and carrots are enhanced here with a simple, spicy garlic sauce. For a twist, try using the new-to-the-market maroon carrot— equally nutritious and flavorful but even more colorful and perhaps a touch sweeter. Maroon carrots are a beautiful beet-like color on the outside and bright orange on the inside, making them visually stunning when sliced or shredded. Find them in large supermarkets and specialty stores.

3 cups fresh broccoli florets
3 cups fresh cauliflower
   florets
1 cup thinly sliced carrot
1 tablespoon butter
3 garlic cloves, chopped
½ teaspoon salt
¼ teaspoon crushed red
   pepper

1. Put the broccoli, cauliflower, and carrot in a steamer basket; set in a saucepan over 1 inch of boiling water. Cover tightly and steam until crisp-tender, 6–8 minutes.
2. Meanwhile, heat a small nonstick skillet over medium heat. Swirl in the butter, then add the garlic. Cook, stirring frequently to keep it from browning, until fragrant, about 3 minutes. Stir in the salt and crushed red pepper.
3. Transfer the vegetables to a serving dish; drizzle with the garlic butter and toss to coat.

Per serving (¾ cup): 50 Cal, 2 g Fat, 1 g Sat Fat, 5 mg Chol, 225 mg Sod, 7 g Carb, 3 g Fib, 2 g Prot, 36 mg Calc. **POINTS: 1.**

 tip These buttery-garlic vegetables are just the right go-along for our Potato and Cheddar Pizza Paysanne (page 84).

Flash-Roasted Bell Peppers and Radicchio

Makes 4 servings

While the pizza is baking, pop these vegetables into the oven to roast at the same time. If your pizza is baking at a temperature lower than 500°F, add a few more minutes to the cooking time. Put the vegetables in the oven about 12 minutes before you expect your pizza to be ready. Substitute other vegetables such as sliced zucchini, summer squash, and mushrooms for the bell peppers and radicchio, if you like.

1 red bell pepper, seeded and cut into eighths
1 yellow bell pepper, seeded and cut into eighths
1 head radicchio, cleaned and cut into 8 wedges
1 medium red onion, cut into eighths
1½ tablespoons chopped fresh rosemary, or 1½ teaspoons dried, crumbled
1 tablespoon olive oil
¾ teaspoon salt
 Freshly ground pepper, to taste

1. Preheat the oven to 500°F. Spray a large nonstick baking pan with nonstick spray.
2. Combine the bell peppers, radicchio, onion, rosemary, oil, salt, and pepper in a large bowl; toss to coat. Arrange the vegetables on the baking pan in a single layer. Roast until lightly browned, turning once, about 12 minutes

Per serving (1 cup): 61 Cal, 4 g Fat, 1 g Sat Fat, 0 mg Chol, 443 mg Sod, 7 g Carb, 2 g Fib, 1 g Prot, 17 mg Calc. **POINTS: 1.**

 tip Leave the radicchio core attached to each wedge, to help hold the wedges intact. Try these roasted vegetables with our Traditional Cheese Pizza (page 78).

Sweet Slices

"Pizzas" for Dessert

Banana-Coconut-Cream
Meringue Pizza

Banana-Coconut-Cream Meringue Pizza

Makes 12 servings

The "crust" for this delicious dessert pizza is a crispy, fat-free meringue. Its crunch contrasts nicely with the creamy custard filling. The meringue can be made a day ahead and stored in an airtight container at room temperature. The custard can be made and kept in the refrigerator for up to two days. Assemble the dessert right before serving.

4 egg whites

¼ teaspoon cream of tartar

¾ cup sugar

1 (3.4-ounce) package sugar-free instant vanilla pudding

1 cup low-fat (1%) milk

1 teaspoon coconut extract

1½ cups light nondairy whipped topping

3 tablespoons apricot jam

1 tablespoon fresh lemon juice

4 ounces semisweet chocolate, melted

5 medium bananas, thinly sliced on the diagonal

2 tablespoons toasted flaked sweetened coconut

1. Preheat the oven to 200°F. Line a 12-inch round pizza pan with foil. Or, line a large baking sheet with foil and use a toothpick to lightly trace a 12-inch circle onto the foil.

2. With an electric mixer at medium speed, beat the egg whites and cream of tartar in a large bowl just until frothy. Gradually beat in the sugar, 2 tablespoons at a time, until the sugar completely dissolves and the whites stand in stiff, glossy peaks, about 8 minutes. Spread the mixture onto the pan, making a 12-inch round with a 1-inch high border around the outer rim. Bake until crisp to the touch, about 3 hours. Turn the oven off and leave the meringue in the oven until it is crisp and dry to the touch, about 30 minutes longer. Let the meringue cool on the pan on a rack for 30 minutes. Carefully loosen and peel off the foil. Gently place the meringue on a serving plate.

3. Meanwhile, to prepare the custard, whisk together the pudding, milk, and coconut extract in a medium bowl until thickened, about 2 minutes. Fold in the whipped topping until just blended. Refrigerate, covered, until chilled, at least 1 hour or up to 2 days.

4. Heat the jam in a small saucepan over low heat until melted; remove from the heat and stir in the lemon juice.

5. To assemble, brush the melted chocolate on the meringue, spreading it to the edge. Spoon the custard over the chocolate. Arrange the banana slices over the custard; brush with the apricot jam mixture, then sprinkle with the coconut.

Per serving (1/12 of pizza): 196 Cal, 5 g Fat, 3 g Sat Fat, 1 mg Chol, 41 mg Sod, 38 g Carb, 2 g Fib, 3 g Prot, 39 mg Calc. *POINTS: 4.*

Blueberry Cobbler Pizza

Makes 8 servings

Any variety of fresh fruits or berries can be used for this tasty cobbler. Substitute pitted sliced plums, peaches, or cherries for the blueberries if you prefer.

3 cups fresh blueberries

6 tablespoons sugar

2 teaspoons grated lemon zest

2¼ cups all-purpose reduced-fat baking mix

¾ teaspoon ground cinnamon

⅛ teaspoon ground nutmeg

¾ cup fat-free milk

2 tablespoons butter, melted

1. Preheat the oven to 375°F. Spray a 10-inch deep-dish pie plate with nonstick spray.
2. Combine the blueberries, 3 tablespoons of the sugar, and the lemon zest in a medium bowl. Spoon the blueberries into the pie plate.
3. Combine the baking mix, the remaining 3 tablespoons sugar, the cinnamon, and nutmeg in a medium bowl. Stir in the milk and butter just until blended. Spoon the batter in 8 even dollops on top of the blueberries. Bake until the filling is hot and the topping is lightly browned, 35–40 minutes. Let the cobbler cool on a rack 10 minutes and serve warm. Or let cool completely on the rack and serve at room temperature.

Per serving (⅛ of cobbler): 227 Cal, 5 g Fat, 2 g Sat Fat, 8 mg Chol, 403 mg Sod, 40 g Carb, 2 g Fib, 4 g Prot, 64 mg Calc. **POINTS: 5.**

 tip Aromatic oils that are naturally present in lemon zest give so much flavor to food. The zest of the lemon is the outermost, colored layer of the skin of the lemon (without any of the bitter white pith underneath the skin). To remove the zest, rub the whole lemon against the fine side of a grater until the thin lemon-colored skin, or zest, is grated away.

Thin and Crispy Peach Pizza Pie

Makes 16 servings

Rolling the chilled dough very thin is what gives you a crispy pie crust here. And because the pastry is very thin and delicate, the peaches need to be thinly sliced, too. If fresh ripe peaches aren't in season, use thinly sliced apples, pears, or plums instead.

CRUST

- 2 cups all-purpose flour
- 1 teaspoon sugar
- ½ teaspoon salt
- 4 tablespoons unsalted butter, chilled and cut into pieces
- 3 tablespoons olive oil
- 5–7 tablespoons ice water

FILLING

- 4 (about 1½ pounds) ripe peaches, peeled, pitted, and thinly sliced
- 3 tablespoons plus 1 teaspoon sugar
- 1 tablespoon fresh lemon juice
- 1 teaspoon almond extract
- 2 teaspoons water

1. To make the crust, pulse the flour, sugar, and salt in a food processor to mix. Add the butter and oil; pulse until the mixture is crumbly. With the machine running, add the water, 1 tablespoon at a time, until the dough forms a ball. Cut the dough in half and flatten each into a 6-inch round. Wrap in plastic wrap and refrigerate until firm, at least 30 minutes.

2. To make the filling, combine the peaches, the 3 tablespoons sugar, the lemon juice, and almond extract in a large bowl; set aside.

3. Place one piece of dough on a lightly floured surface. With a floured rolling pin, roll into a 12-inch circle. Place the dough on a large baking sheet. Arrange the peach mixture on the dough, leaving a 1-inch border.

4. Preheat the oven to 400°F. Roll out the remaining dough to a 13-inch circle. Place the dough over the peach filling. Crimp the edge of the dough with a fork so the top crust adheres to the bottom crust. Brush the top with the water and sprinkle with the remaining 1 teaspoon sugar. Make a few slits in the crust with a small sharp knife, to allow steam to escape. Bake until the filling is hot and the crust is golden, 50–55 minutes. Serve warm or at room temperature.

Per serving (1/16 of pie): 131 Cal, 6 g Fat, 2 g Sat Fat, 8 mg Chol, 74 mg Sod, 18 g Carb, 1 g Fib, 2 g Prot, 5 mg Calc. **POINTS: 3.**

 tip The dough can be placed in a zip-close plastic freezer bag and frozen for up to two weeks. Thaw overnight in the refrigerator.

Taffy Apple Pizza

Makes 12 servings

Gooey taffy apples top a flaky phyllo crust, giving new meaning to this favorite autumn treat. Use a combination of your favorite apples, or if you like, substitute an equal amount of pears for the apples.

2 Granny Smith apples, peeled and thinly sliced

3 tablespoons + 1 teaspoon sugar

1 tablespoon all-purpose flour

1 tablespoon fresh lemon juice

1¼ teaspoons ground cinnamon

2 tablespoons chopped pecans

6 (14 × 18-inch) sheets phyllo dough, thawed according to package directions

1 tablespoon butter, melted

3 tablespoons store-bought caramel sauce

1. Combine the apples, the 3 tablespoons sugar, the flour, lemon juice, and 1 teaspoon of the cinnamon in a bowl; set aside.
2. Combine the pecans with the remaining 1 teaspoon sugar and the remaining ¼ teaspoon cinnamon in a small bowl; set aside.
3. Preheat the oven to 375°F. Spray a 12-inch pizza pan or large baking sheet with nonstick spray. As you work, keep the sheets of phyllo covered with plastic wrap to keep them from drying out. Lay one sheet of phyllo across the pizza pan; lightly spray with nonstick spray. Repeat layering the remaining 5 sheets of phyllo, spraying each sheet lightly with nonstick spray. Roll the edges of the phyllo in to make a rimmed edge.
4. Arrange the apple mixture in concentric circles on the phyllo. Brush the apples with the melted butter, then sprinkle with the pecan mixture. Bake until the edges of the phyllo are golden brown and the apples are tender, about 45 minutes. Let cool on the pan on a rack 30 minutes, then drizzle with the caramel sauce.

Per serving (¹⁄₁₂ of pizza): 95 Cal, 3 g Fat, 1 g Sat Fat, 3 mg Chol, 61 mg Sod, 18 g Carb, 1 g Fib, 1 g Prot, 9 mg Calc. *POINTS: 2.*

 tip Phyllo dough, found in the freezer section of your supermarket, must be fully thawed before using. It is very fragile and can dry out quickly after opening, so keep the dough covered with plastic wrap as you work. Follow the package directions for storage.

Taffy Apple Pizza

Chocolate Strawberry Shortcake

Makes 8 servings

Chocolate shortcake, topped with juicy strawberries fragrantly spiked with fresh mint, is a treat for both chocolate lovers and strawberry lovers. If you like, use your own berry combination—raspberries, blueberries, and blackberries. Even slices of fresh peaches or nectarines would be good here.

2 cups all-purpose reduced-fat baking mix

½ cup sugar

¼ cup sifted unsweetened cocoa powder

⅔ cup low-fat (1%) milk

3 tablespoons reduced-calorie margarine, melted

4 cups fresh strawberries, hulled and sliced

2 tablespoons orange juice

1 tablespoon chopped fresh mint

8 tablespoons light nondairy whipped topping

8 fresh mint sprigs, for garnish

1. Preheat the oven to 425°F. Spray a 10-inch pie dish with nonstick spray.

2. Combine the baking mix, 6 tablespoons of the sugar, the cocoa, milk, and margarine in a medium bowl; stir until blended. Scrape the batter into the pie dish.

3. Bake until a toothpick inserted in the center comes out clean, 20–25 minutes. Let cool in the pie dish on a rack 5 minutes. Remove the shortcake from the pie dish and let cool on the rack, about 10 minutes.

4. Meanwhile, combine the strawberries, the remaining 2 tablespoons sugar, the orange juice, and chopped mint in a large bowl.

5. Place the shortcake on a large plate. Spoon the strawberry mixture over the shortcake. Cut into 8 wedges. Serve each wedge with 1 tablespoon of the whipped topping and garnish with a mint sprig.

Per serving (1 wedge with 1 tablespoon topping): 222 Cal, 5 g Fat, 1 g Sat Fat, 1 mg Chol, 362 mg Sod, 41 g Carb, 3 g Fib, 4 g Prot, 69 mg Calc. **POINTS: 4.**

 **CUT POINTS** Stretch this dessert to 10 servings and you'll save just about *1 POINT.*

S'mores Cookie Pizza

Makes 10 servings

Gooey wedges of this all-American favorite will satisfy any sweet-tooth craving and make a perfect lunch box treat or after-school snack. The yogurt spread comes in tubs and can be found near the butter in the supermarket.

12 full sheets (48 crackers) reduced-fat graham crackers, broken into pieces

¼ cup reduced-calorie yogurt spread

2 tablespoons sugar

1¼ cups mini marshmallows

¼ cup semisweet mini chocolate chips

2 tablespoons fat-free chocolate syrup

1. Preheat the oven to 375°F. Spray a 9-inch springform pan with nonstick spray.
2. Pulse the graham crackers, yogurt spread, and sugar in a food processor until fine crumbs form. Press the crumb mixture into the bottom of the pan. Bake until just set, about 10 minutes. Remove the pan from the oven, then reduce the oven temperature to 350°F.
3. Sprinkle the marshmallows and the chocolate chips onto the crust. Bake until the marshmallows are lightly browned, about 15 minutes. Let cool 15 minutes, then drizzle the top with the chocolate syrup.

Per serving (¹⁄₁₀ of pizza): 193 Cal, 5 g Fat, 1 g Sat Fat, 0 mg Chol, 230 mg Sod, 38 g Carb, 1 g Fib, 2 g Prot, 10 mg Calc. **POINTS: 4.**

Fudge Brownie Sundae Pie

Fudge Brownie Sundae Pie

Makes 12 servings

Imagine savoring a delectably indulgent combination of creamy chocolate and vanilla frozen yogurt with a rich chocolate brownie in every mouthful. It's a chocolate lover's fantasy come true.

1 (1 pound 4.5-ounce) box reduced-fat fudge brownie mix

⅔ cup water

1 pint fat-free vanilla frozen yogurt

1 pint fat-free chocolate frozen yogurt

3 reduced-fat chocolate sandwich cookies, finely crushed

1. Preheat the oven to 350°F. Spray a 10-inch springform pan with nonstick spray.
2. Combine the brownie mix and water in a large bowl. Scrape the batter into the pan. Bake until a toothpick inserted 2 inches from the side of the pan comes out clean, 30–35 minutes. Let cool in the pan completely on a rack. Leave the baked brownie in the pan.
3. Place the vanilla and chocolate frozen yogurt in the refrigerator to soften slightly, about 15 minutes.
4. Spread the vanilla frozen yogurt on top of the cooled brownie, then spread the softened chocolate frozen yogurt over the top. Sprinkle with the crushed cookies. Cover with plastic wrap and freeze until firm, at least 6 hours or overnight.
5. Run a knife or metal spatula, dipped in hot water, around the inside rim of the springform pan to loosen the pie. Remove the outer rim of the pan, then place the pie on a large plate. Let the pie stand 15 minutes at room temperature before slicing and serving.

Per serving (¹⁄₁₂ of pie): 225 Cal, 4 g Fat, 1 g Sat Fat, 1 mg Chol, 203 mg Sod, 46 g Carb, 2 g Fib, 4 g Prot, 77 mg Calc. ***POINTS: 4.***

Custard Phyllo Pie

Makes 20 servings

Because this has a custard filling, let it sit at room temperature for no more than two hours, then refrigerate any leftovers.

4 cups low-fat (1%) milk
½ cup farina
⅓ cup plus ¾ cup sugar
¼ teaspoon salt
1 cup fat-free egg substitute
1 tablespoon grated orange zest
1 teaspoon vanilla extract
1 cup water
1 cinnamon stick
2 whole cloves
2 teaspoons fresh lemon juice
12 (14 × 18-inch) sheets phyllo dough, thawed according to package directions

1. To prepare the filling, combine the milk, farina, the ⅓ cup sugar, and the salt in a medium saucepan; bring to a boil, stirring frequently. Reduce the heat and simmer, uncovered, stirring frequently, until the mixture is thick and creamy, about 12 minutes. Remove from the heat and slowly stir in the egg substitute, orange zest, and vanilla. Set aside to cool, 15 minutes.

2. To prepare the syrup, bring the water, the remaining ¾ cup sugar, the cinnamon stick, and cloves to a boil in a small saucepan. Reduce the heat and simmer, stirring occasionally, until the sugar dissolves and the mixture thickens slightly, about 10 minutes. Remove from the heat; stir in the lemon juice. Set aside to cool. Preheat the oven to 350°F. Spray a 9 × 13-inch nonstick baking pan with nonstick spray.

3. Keep the phyllo covered with plastic wrap to prevent drying out. Lay one sheet of phyllo in the baking pan; lightly spray with nonstick spray. Repeat, layering with 5 more sheets of phyllo, spraying each sheet lightly with nonstick spray. Pour in the cooled custard. Cover with the remaining 6 sheets of phyllo, spraying each sheet lightly with nonstick spray. Roll the edges of the phyllo in to make a rimmed edge. With a sharp knife, score the top layers of the phyllo (do not score into the filling) to form 20 squares. Bake until golden and the filling is set, about 45 minutes. Transfer the pan to a rack.

4. Discard the cinnamon stick and cloves from the cooled syrup, then pour the syrup over the pie. Let cool in the pan on the rack, about 30 minutes. Cut into 20 squares. Serve warm or at room temperature.

Per serving (1 square): 128 Cal, 1 g Fat, 0 g Sat Fat, 2 mg Chol, 114 mg Sod, 25 g Carb, 1 g Fib, 4 g Prot, 67 mg Calc. **POINTS: 2.**

Cannoli Pie

Makes 16 servings

A great Italian tradition—cannoli—is the inspiration for this simple, no-bake dessert, with a sweet, creamy ricotta filling and a chocolate cookie crust. For a Neapolitan-style cannoli filling, substitute candied citron for some, or all, of the chocolate chips.

23 reduced-fat chocolate
   sandwich cookies
3 tablespoons reduced-
   calorie yogurt spread
½ cup sugar
1 packet unflavored gelatin
½ cup water
1 (15-ounce) container
   part-skim ricotta cheese
1 teaspoon vanilla extract
½ teaspoon ground
   cinnamon
⅛ teaspoon ground nutmeg
1 cup light nondairy
   whipped topping
2 tablespoons mini
   semisweet chocolate
   chips
2 tablespoons
   confectioners' sugar

1. Place the cookies in a food processor and pulse until fine crumbs form, about 1 minute. Add the yogurt spread and pulse until the mixture is well blended. Press the crumb mixture onto the bottom of a 10-inch springform pan. Refrigerate the crust while preparing the filling.

2. Meanwhile, place the sugar and gelatin in a small bowl. Bring the water to a boil in a small saucepan. Pour the water over the sugar mixture, stirring constantly, until the sugar and gelatin completely dissolve; set aside.

3. Puree the ricotta cheese, vanilla, cinnamon, and nutmeg in a food processor. Transfer to a bowl. Stir in the gelatin mixture, then gently fold in the whipped topping. Spoon the ricotta mixture onto the crust, then sprinkle with the chocolate chips. Refrigerate until set, at least 3 hours.

4. Run a knife or metal spatula, dipped in hot water, around the inside rim of the springform pan to loosen the pie. Remove the outer rim of the pan, then place the pie on a large plate. Sprinkle with the confectioners' sugar just before serving.

Per serving (1/16 of pie): 155 Cal, 5 g Fat, 3 g Sat Fat, 8 mg Chol, 136 mg Sod, 21 g Carb, 0 g Fib, 4 g Prot, 84 mg Calc. **POINTS: 4.**

Giant Linzer Cookie

Makes 12 servings

Four simple ingredients combine here to form a sweet treat of flaky almond shortbread with a jewel-like raspberry topping. If you like, substitute any other fruit spread—such as strawberry, apricot, or peach—for the raspberry spread. Or top half of the cookie crust with one fruit spread and the other half with another. It's perfect with an afternoon cup of tea.

20 reduced-fat, sugar-free shortbread cookies

3 tablespoons reduced-calorie yogurt spread

3 tablespoons sliced almonds

1 (10-ounce) jar seedless raspberry fruit spread

1. Preheat the oven to 375°F. Spray a 9-inch nonstick springform pan with nonstick spray.

2. Pulse the cookies, the reduced-calorie spread, and 2 tablespoons of the almonds in a food processor until finely crushed, about 10 seconds. Reserve $\frac{1}{4}$ cup of the cookie mixture. Press the remaining cookie mixture into the bottom of the pan. Bake 10 minutes. Remove the pan from the oven.

3. Spoon the raspberry fruit spread over the top of the crust. Sprinkle with the remaining $\frac{1}{4}$ cup cookie mixture and top with the remaining 1 tablespoon almonds. Return the pan to the oven and bake until the fruit spread begins to bubble around the edges, about 10 minutes. Let cool in the pan on a rack, about 20 minutes. Refrigerate in the pan until the filling is set, about 30 minutes longer.

4. Run a knife or metal spatula around the inside rim of the springform pan to loosen the sides of the cookie. Remove the outer rim of the pan, then place the cookie on a large plate.

Per serving ($\frac{1}{12}$ of cookie): 150 Cal, 5 g Fat, 1 g Sat Fat, 3 mg Chol, 108 mg Sod, 27 g Carb, 2 g Fib, 2 g Prot, 12 mg Calc. *POINTS: 3.*

Giant Linzer Cookie

Index

A

Amatriciana Topping, 165
anchovy(ies):
    Onion, and Olive Pizza, 64
    Pissaladière Bruschetta, 153
    Pizza Pissaladière, Classic, 20
antipasto:
    Salad, 182
    -Stuffed Focaccia, 16
apple:
    Avocado, and Grapefruit with Poppy Seed Dressing, 186, 187
    Taffy, Pizza, 206, 207
artichoke(s):
    Hearts, in Instant Moroccan Topping, 171
    Pesto Topping, 166
    Seafood Pizza with, 67
    and Tomato Pizza Pronto, 157
arugula:
    and Pesto-Scallop Pizza, 70
    Seared-Salmon Pizzas with Shaved Parmesan and, 68, 69
asparagus:
    Pizza Primavera, 100, 101
    Primavera Sauté, 196
    Turkey Alfredo-Saltimbocca Pizza with, 40
avocado:
    Corn, and Tomato Muffin Pizzas, 158
    Grapefruit, and Apple with Poppy Seed Dressing, 186, 187

B

bacon:
    Amatriciana Topping, 165
    Canadian, and Pear Pizza, Grilled, 125
    Canadian, in Pizza Rustica, 108, 109
    Spinach and Radish Salad with, Warm, 184
    Three-Mushroom, and Onion Pizza, 112
baking pizza, tips for, 8
Balsamic Eggplant and Feta Pitzas, Grilled, 136
Banana-Coconut-Cream Meringue Pizza, 202, 203
Barbecued Chicken Pizzas, 54
Basic Pizza Dough, 10
basil:
    Tomato Dressing, Mixed Greens with, 183
    see also pesto
bean(s):

pinto, in Seven-Layer Taco Pizzas, 93
    Red, and Escarole Pitzas, 94
    see also black bean(s); white bean(s)
beef:
    corned, in Deli Fast-Track Reuben Pizza, 156
    Pizza Bolognese, 48
    Steak Lovers' Grilled Pizza, 120, 121
    Tex-Mex Tostada Pizzas with Black Beans and, 53
Beet and Fennel Salad with Chive Vinaigrette, 190
Belgian Endive with Pear and Cilantro Topping, 185
Biscuit-Crust Pizza, Sausage and Pepperoni, 41
black bean(s):
    Hummus Pita Pizza, 149
    and Shrimp Topping, 170
    Tex-Mex Tostada Pizzas with Beef and, 53
Blueberry Cobbler Pizza, 204
Bolognese Pizza, 48
broccoli:
    and Sausage Calzones, 45
    Steamed Fall Vegetables with Garlic, 197
    and Sun-Dried Tomato Pizza, Spicy, 113
Brownie, Fudge, Sundae Pie, 210, 211
bruschetta:
    Pissaladière, 153
    San Francisco Roasted Pepper, 150, 151
    Tapenade, Goat Cheese, and Tomato, 154
    Tomato, Slices, 33
Buffalo Chicken Pizzas, 52

C

cabbage, in Minted Slaw with Orange and Cranberries, 188
Caesar-Salad Chicken Pitzas, 49
Cajun Sausage Pizza, New Orleans, 50, 51
California Pizzettes with Smoked Chicken and Sun-Dried Tomato Pesto, 36
California Sausage, Pepper, and Onion Pizza, 128
calzones:
    Greek Skillet, 88
    Mini, with Goat Cheese and Figs, 26
    Pastrami Reuben, 116
    Sausage and Broccoli, 45
Canadian bacon:
    and Pear Pizza, Grilled, 125
    Pizza Rustica, 108, 109
Cannoli Pie, 213
caponata:
    Topping, 172
    and White Bean Pizza, 147

Note: Page numbers in *italics* refer to photographs.

carrots:
  Mixed Vegetable Pickles, 194
  Steamed Fall Vegetables with Garlic, 197
cauliflower:
  Mashed, Topping, 173
  Mixed Vegetable Pickles, 194
  Steamed Fall Vegetables with Garlic, 197
Cheddar and Potato Pizza Paysanne, 84, *85*
cheese:
  Pizza, Traditional, 78
  Smoked, Flatbread with Smoked Ham and, 17
  Spread, Roast-Garlic, Herbed Flatbreads with, *18,* 19
  Three-, and Roasted-Garlic Pizza Strips, 30
  Two-, Greek Pizza, 144
  see also specific cheeses
Chicago Pizza with Ham, Cheese, and Roasted Peppers,
  38, 39
chicken:
  Barbecued, Pizzas, 54
  Buffalo, Pizzas, 52
  Caesar-Salad Pitzas, 49
  Chipotle Pizza, 107
  Corn, and Manchego Pizza, 126, *127*
  Hot and Spicy Mexican Tortillizzas, 145
  Moroccan Pita Pizzas, 152
  Pizza Française, 46, *47*
  Sage, and Pepper Pizza, 122
  Smoked, California Pizzettes with Sun-Dried Tomato
    Pesto and, 36
  South-of-the-Border Pizza, 148
chipotle:
  Chicken Pizza, 107
  Tomato Salsa, Nacho Pizzas with, 22, *23*
Chive Vinaigrette, Beet and Fennel Salad with, 190
chocolate:
  Cannoli Pie, 213
  Fudge Brownie Sundae Pie, *210,* 211
  S'mores Cookie Pizza, 209
  Strawberry Shortcake, 208
cilantro:
  Green and White Tortillizzas, Simple, 146
  and Pear Topping, Belgian Endive with, 185
Clam Pizza, White, 66
Coastal Pizza, 132, *133*
Cobbler Pizza, Blueberry, 204
Coconut-Cream-Banana Meringue Pizza, *202,* 203
cookie(s):
  Linzer, Giant, 214, *215*
  S'mores, Pizza, 209

corn:
  Avocado, and Tomato Muffin Pizzas, 158
  Chicken, and Manchego Pizza, 126, *127*
  Mixed Vegetable Pickles, 194
corned beef, in Deli Fast-Track Reuben Pizza, 156
Cornmeal Pizza Dough, 11
Cranberries, Minted Slaw with Orange and, 188
creating your own pizza, 179
Creole Pizza, Shrimp, 60
Cucumber, Tomato, and Mozzarella Salad,
  Chunky, 191
Curried Vegetable Pizza, 89
Custard Phyllo Pie, 212

D

deep-dish pizzas:
  Chicago, with Ham, Cheese, and Roasted
    Peppers, *38,* 39
  Mussels Fra Diavolo, *62,* 63
  Roasted Vegetable and "Soysage," 83
  Scallop and Spinach, 61
Deli Fast-Track Reuben Pizza, 156
dessert "pizzas," 200–215
  Banana-Coconut-Cream Meringue, *202,* 203
  Blueberry Cobbler, 204
  Cannoli Pie, 213
  Chocolate Strawberry Shortcake, 208
  Custard Phyllo Pie, 212
  Fudge Brownie Sundae Pie, *210,* 211
  Linzer Cookie, Giant, 214, *215*
  Peach Pie, Thin and Crispy, 205
  S'mores Cookie, 209
  Taffy Apple, 206, *207*
Duck, Herbed, and Tomato Pizza, 124

E

eggplant:
  Balsamic, and Feta Pitzas, Grilled, 136
  Caponata Topping, 172
  Grilled Summer Vegetables with Fresh Salsa, 195
  Mediterranean Pan Pizza, 110
English muffins:
  Artichoke and Tomato Pizza Pronto, 157
  Avocado, Corn, and Tomato Muffin Pizzas, 158
  Barbecued Chicken Pizzas, 54
  Piquillo Pepper Pizzettes, 79
  Summer Garden Pizzettes, 32
  Tuna-Tomato Pizza Melts, 75
Escarole and Red Bean Pitzas, 94

F

Fennel and Beet Salad with Chive Vinaigrette, 190
feta:
    and Balsamic Eggplant Pitzas, Grilled, 136
    Dressing, Creamy, Greek Salad Pizza with, 106
    Greek Island Pitzas, 31
    Moroccan Topping, Instant, 171
    Spanakopizza, 103
    Two-Cheese Greek Pizza, 144
fig(s):
    Caramelized Onion, and Stilton Pizza, *90,* 91
    Mini Calzones with Goat Cheese and, 26
flatbreads:
    Herbed, with Roast-Garlic Cheese Spread, *18,* 19
    Lemon-Thyme Zucchini on, 135
    with Sausage and Peppers, *114,* 115
    with Smoked Ham and Cheese, 17
focaccia:
    Antipasto-Stuffed, 16
    Sesame, Shallot, and Thyme, 87
    Stuffed Pizza, 142, *143*
French bread:
    New Orleans Cajun Sausage Pizza, *50,* 51
    Tomato Bruschetta Slices, 33
Fudge Brownie Sundae Pie, *210,* 211

G

Galette, Plum Tomato, 27
garlic:
    Potato and Caramelized Onion Pizza, 111
    Roast-, Cheese Spread, Herbed Flatbreads with, *18,* 19
    Roasted-, and Three-Cheese Pizza Strips, 30
    Rosemary Pepperonata Topping, 162
    Steamed Fall Vegetables with, 197
Giant Linzer Cookie, 214, *215*
Giant Popover Portobello Pizza, 92
goat cheese:
    Lobster, and Sun-Dried Tomato Pizza, 59
    Mini Calzones with Figs and, 26
    Pissaladière Squares with Tomato Coulis and, *80,* 81
    Roasted Onion and Olive Pizza with, 99
    Tapenade, and Tomato Bruschetta, 154
    Three-Cheese and Roasted-Garlic Pizza Strips, 30
Grapefruit, Avocado, and Apple with Poppy Seed Dressing, *186,* 187
Greek flavors:
    Greek Island Pitzas, 31
    Greek Salad Pizza with Creamy Feta Dressing, 106

    Skillet Calzones, 88
    Spanakopizza, 103
    Two-Cheese Pizza, 144
Green and White Tortillizzas, Simple, 146
grilled pizzas, 118–139
    Balsamic Eggplant and Feta Pitzas, 136
    Canadian Bacon and Pear, 125
    Chicken, Corn, and Manchego, 126, *127*
    Coastal, 132, *133*
    guidelines for, 138
    Herbed Duck and Tomato, 124
    Lemon-Thyme Zucchini on Flatbread, 135
    Pork and Poblano-Pepper, 137
    Radicchio and Shiitake Pizza, 129
    Sage Chicken and Pepper, 122
    Sausage, Pepper, and Onion, California, 128
    Sausage and White Bean, Spicy, 130
    Shrimp, Hummus, and Red Pepper, 134
    Smoked Turkey, Grilled Onion, and Tomato, 123
    Steak Lovers', *120,* 121
    tools for, 139
    Tortilla, Spanish, 131
Grilled Summer Vegetables with Fresh Salsa, 195

H

ham:
    Chicago Pizza with Cheese, Roasted Peppers and, *38,* 39
    Grilled Spanish Tortilla Pizza, 131
    and Mushroom Toasts with Red Pesto, 155
    Smoked, Flatbread with Cheese and, 17
herbed:
    Duck and Tomato Pizza, 124
    Flatbreads with Roast-Garlic Cheese Spread, *18,* 19
hummus:
    Black Bean, Pita Pizza, 149
    Moroccan Pita Pizza, 152
    Shrimp, and Red Pepper Pizza, 134

I

Individual Salad Pizzas, 86
Italian bread:
    Ham and Mushroom Toasts with Red Pesto, 155
    Pissaladière Bruschetta, 153
    Pizza Loaf, 95
    Pizza with Sardines, 71
    Shrimp, Hummus, and Red Pepper Pizza, 134
    Tapenade, Goat Cheese, and Tomato Bruschetta, 154

J

Jarlsberg cheese:
Deli Fast-Track Reuben Pizza, 156
Pastrami Reuben Calzones, 116
Pizza with Caramelized Leeks, *104,* 105
Jicama and Tomato Salad, 189

L

lavash:
Flatbreads with Sausage and Peppers, *114,* 115
Seared-Salmon Pizzas with Arugula and Shaved
Parmesan, *68,* 69
Leeks, Caramelized, Pizza with, *104,* 105
Lemon-Thyme Zucchini on Flatbread, 135
Linzer Cookie, Giant, 214, *215*
Loaf, Pizza, 95
Lobster, Goat Cheese, and Sun-Dried Tomato Pizza, 59

M

manchego:
Chicken, and Corn Pizza, 126, *127*
Grilled Spanish Tortilla Pizza, 131
Margherita Pizza with Roasted Grape Tomatoes, 82
Mediterranean Pan Pizza, 110
Meringue Pizza, Banana-Coconut-Cream, *202,* 203
Mexican and Tex-Mex flavors:
Black Bean Hummus Pita Pizza, 149
Hot and Spicy Mexican Tortillizzas, 145
Jicama and Tomato Salad, 189
Mini Mexi-Pizzas with Sole, 74
Nacho Pizzas with Fresh Chipotle-Tomato
Salsa, 22, *23*
Pizza Grande, 98
Pork Taco Pizzas, Spicy, *42,* 43
Seven-Layer Taco Pizzas, 93
Smoked Turkey, Grilled Onion, and Tomato Pizza, 123
South-of-the-Border Pizza, 148
Tostada Pizzas with Beef and Black Beans, 53
Minted Slaw with Orange and Cranberries, 188
Mixed Greens with Tomato-Basil Dressing, 183
Moroccan flavors:
Pita Pizzas, 152
Topping, Instant, 171
Mozzarella, Tomato, and Cucumber Salad, Chunky, 191
mushroom(s):
Caponata Topping, 172
Double, Topping, 174, *175*
Focaccia Stuffed Pizza, 142, *143*

and Ham Toasts with Red Pesto, 155
Portobello Pizza, Giant Popover, 92
Roasted Vegetable Sauce Topping, 177
Shiitake and Radicchio Pizza, Grilled, 129
Three-, Onion, and Bacon Pizza, 112
Mussels Fra Diavolo Pizza, Deep-Dish, *62,* 63

N

Nacho Pizzas with Fresh Chipotle-Tomato Salsa, 22, *23*
New Orleans Cajun Sausage Pizza, *50,* 51

O

olive(s):
Anchovy, and Onion Pizza, 64
Pizza Pissaladière, Classic, 20
and Roasted Onion Pizza with Goat Cheese, 99
Tapenade, Goat Cheese, and Tomato Bruschetta, 154
Tuna, and Roasted Pepper Pizza, 65
onion(s):
Anchovy, and Olive Pizza, 64
Caramelized, and Potato Pizza, Garlicky, 111
Caramelized, Fig, and Stilton Pizza, *90,* 91
Caramelized, Topping, 176
Grilled, Smoked Turkey, and Tomato Pizza, 123
Pizza Pissaladière, Classic, 20
Roasted, and Olive Pizza with Goat Cheese, 99
Sausage, and Pepper Pizza, California, 128
Steak Lovers' Grilled Pizza, *120,* 121
Three-Mushroom, and Bacon Pizza, 112
orange:
Minted Slaw with Cranberries and, 188
and Tomato Stacks, 192, *193*

P

Parmesan, Shaved, Seared-Salmon Pizzas with Arugula
and, *68,* 69
Pastrami Reuben Calzones, 116
Peach Pizza Pie, Thin and Crispy, 205
pear:
and Canadian Bacon Pizza, Grilled, 125
and Cilantro Topping, Belgian Endive with, 185
pepper(s):
Bell, Flash-Roasted Radicchio and, 198, *199*
Flatbreads with Sausage and, *114,* 115
Focaccia Stuffed Pizza, 142, *143*
Mixed-, Pizza Wedges, Spicy, 24
Piquillo, Pizzettes, 79
Pizza Loaf, 95

Poblano, and Pork Pizza, 137
Red, Shrimp, and Hummus Pizza, 134
Roasted, Bruschetta, San Francisco, *150,* 151
Roasted, Chicago Pizza with Ham, Cheese and,
    38, 39
Roasted, Tuna, and Olive Pizza, 65
Roasted Vegetable Sauce Topping, 177
Roasted Yellow, Pesto Pizza with Tomatoes and, 102
Rosemary-Garlic Pepperonata Topping, 162
and Sage Chicken Pizza, 122
Sausage, and Onion Pizza, California, 128
Pepperonata Topping, Rosemary-Garlic, 162
Pepperoni and Sausage Biscuit-Crust Pizza, 41
pesto:
    Artichoke Topping, 166
    Pizza with Roasted Yellow Peppers and
        Tomatoes, 102
    Red, Ham and Mushroom Toasts with, 155
    -Scallop and Arugula Pizza, 70
    Sun-Dried Tomato, California Pizzettes with Smoked
        Chicken and, 36
phyllo:
    Pie, Custard, 212
    Plum Tomato Galette, 27
    Taffy Apple Pizza, 206, *207*
Pickles, Mixed Vegetable, 194
pies:
    Cannoli, 213
    Custard Phyllo, 212
    Fudge Brownie Sundae, *210,* 211
    Peach Pizza, Thin and Crispy, 205
pinto beans, in Seven-Layer Taco Pizzas, 93
Piquillo Pepper Pizzettes, 79
pissaladière:
    Bruschetta, 153
    Pizza, Classic, 20
    Squares with Tomato Coulis and Goat Cheese, *80,* 81
pita pizzas (pitzas):
    Balsamic Eggplant and Feta, Grilled, 136
    Black Bean Hummus, 149
    Chicken Caesar-Salad, 49
    Greek Island, 31
    Moroccan, 152
    Red Bean and Escarole, 94
pizza doughs:
    Basic, 10
    Cornmeal, 11
    Semolina, 11
    tips for, 8

Whole-Wheat, 11
pizzettes:
    California, with Smoked Chicken and Sun-Dried
        Tomato Pesto, 36
    Piquillo Pepper, 79
    Summer Garden, 32
Poblano-Pepper and Pork Pizza, 137
Popover Portobello Pizza, Giant, 92
Poppy Seed Dressing, Avocado, Grapefruit, and Apple
    with, *186,* 187
pork:
    and Poblano-Pepper Pizza, 137
    Satay Pizza, Thai, 44
    Taco Pizzas, Spicy, *42,* 43
    see also bacon; ham; sausage
Portobello Pizza, Giant Popover, 92
potato:
    and Caramelized Onion Pizza, Garlicky, 111
    and Cheddar Pizza Paysanne, 84, *85*
    Rosemary Pizza, Tuna Niçoise on, 58
primavera:
    Pizza, *100,* 101
    Sauté, 196

R
radicchio:
    Flash-Roasted Bell Peppers and, 198, *199*
    and Shiitake Pizza, Grilled, 129
Radish and Spinach Salad with Bacon, Warm, 184
Red Bean and Escarole Pitzas, 94
Reuben:
    Deli Fast-Track, Pizza, 156
    Pastrami, Calzones, 116
Ricotta and Spinach Topping, Spiced, 163
rosemary:
    Garlic Pepperonata Topping, 162
    Potato Pizza, Tuna Niçoise on, 58
Rustica, Pizza, 108, *109*

S
Sage Chicken and Pepper Pizza, 122
salad(s), 182–193
    Antipasto, 182
    Avocado, Grapefruit, and Apple with Poppy Seed
        Dressing, *186,* 187
    Beet and Fennel, with Chive Vinaigrette, 190
    Belgian Endive with Pear and Cilantro Topping, 185
    Greek, Pizza, with Creamy Feta Dressing, 106
    Jicama and Tomato, 189

Minted Slaw with Orange and Cranberries, 188
Mixed Greens with Tomato-Basil Dressing, 183
Pizzas, Individual, 86
Spinach and Radish, with Bacon, Warm, 184
Tomato, Cucumber, and Mozzarella, Chunky, 191
Tomato and Orange Stacks, 192, *193*
salmon:
Coastal Pizza, 132, *133*
Seared-, Pizzas with Arugula and Shaved Parmesan, *68,* 69
Smoked, Pizza Slices with Wasabi Cream and Chives, 21
salsa:
Chipotle-Tomato, Nacho Pizzas with, 22, *23*
Fresh, Grilled Summer Vegetables with, 195
San Francisco Roasted Pepper Bruschetta, *150,* 151
Sardines, Italian Bread Pizza with, 71
Satay, Thai Pork, Pizza, 44
sauce(s):
Roasted Vegetable, Topping, 177
Tomato, Basic, 12
Tomato, Roasted, 13
sauerkraut:
Deli Fast-Track Reuben Pizza, 156
Pastrami Reuben Calzones, 116
sausage:
and Broccoli Calzones, 45
Flatbreads with Peppers and, *114,* 115
Pepper, and Onion Pizza, California, 128
and Pepperoni Biscuit-Crust Pizza, 41
Pizza, New Orleans Cajun, *50,* 51
-and-Shrimp Pizzas, Southwestern, 72, *73*
-Stuffed Pizza, Sicilian, 37
and White Bean Pizza, Spicy, 130
scallop:
Pesto-, and Arugula Pizza, 70
and Spinach Pizza, Deep-Dish, 61
Seafood Pizza with Artichokes, 67
Semolina Pizza Dough, 11
Sesame, Shallot, and Thyme Focaccia, 87
shiitake:
Double Mushroom Topping, 174, *175*
and Radicchio Pizza, Grilled, 129
Shortcake, Chocolate Strawberry, 208
shrimp:
and Black Bean Topping, 170
Creole Pizza, 60
Hummus, and Red Pepper Pizza, 134
-and-Sausage Pizzas, Southwestern, 72, *73*

Sicilian Sausage-Stuffed Pizza, 37
side dishes, 194–199
Bell Peppers and Radicchio, Flash-Roasted, 198, *199*
Grilled Summer Vegetables with Fresh Salsa, 195
Mixed Vegetable Pickles, 194
Primavera Sauté, 196
Steamed Fall Vegetables with Garlic, 197
see also salad(s)
Slaw, Minted, with Orange and Cranberries, 188
S'mores Cookie Pizza, 209
Sole, Mini Mexi-Pizzas with, 74
South-of-the-Border Pizza, 148
Southwestern flavors:
Shrimp-and-Sausage Pizzas, 72, *73*
see also Mexican and Tex-Mex flavors
"Soysage" and Roasted Vegetable Deep-Dish Pizza, 83
Spanakopizza, 103
Spanish Tortilla Pizza, Grilled, 131
spinach:
and Radish Salad with Bacon, Warm, 184
and Ricotta Topping, Spiced, 163
and Scallop Pizza, Deep-Dish, 61
Spanakopizza, 103
Two-Cheese Greek Pizza, 144
Steak Lovers' Grilled Pizza, *120,* 121
Stilton, Caramelized Onion, and Fig Pizza, *90,* 91
Strawberry Shortcake, Chocolate, 208
Stromboli Slices, Spicy, 25
Summer Garden Pizzettes, 32
surimi, in Seafood Pizza with Artichokes, 67

T

taco pizzas:
Pork, Spicy, *42,* 43
Seven-Layer, 93
Taffy Apple Pizza, 206, *207*
Tapenade, Goat Cheese, and Tomato Bruschetta, 154
Tex-Mex flavors, *see* Mexican and Tex-Mex flavors
Thai Pork Satay Pizza, 44
thyme:
Lemon Zucchini on Flatbread, 135
Sesame, and Shallot Focaccia, 87
timeline for pizza, 117
tomato(es):
and Artichoke Pizza Pronto, 157
Avocado, and Corn Muffin Pizzas, 158
Basil Dressing, Mixed Greens with, 183
Bruschetta Slices, 33
Chipotle Salsa, Nacho Pizzas with, 22, *23*

Compote Topping, Winter, 178
Coulis, Pissaladière Squares with Goat Cheese and, *80,* 81
Cucumber, and Mozzarella Salad, Chunky, 191
Grape, Roasted, Pizza Margherita with, 82
and Herbed Duck Pizza, 124
and Jicama Salad, 189
and Orange Stacks, 192, *193*
Pesto Pizza with Roasted Yellow Peppers and, 102
Pissaladière Bruschetta, 153
Plum, Galette, 27
Roasted, Sauce, 13
Roasted Plum, Topping, 164
Sauce, Basic, 12
Smoked Turkey, and Grilled Onion Pizza, 123
Sun-Dried, and Broccoli Pizza, Spicy, 113
Sun-Dried, Lobster, and Goat Cheese Pizza, 59
Sun-Dried, Pesto, California Pizzettes with Smoked Chicken and, 36
Tapenade, and Goat Cheese Bruschetta, 154
Tuna Pizza Melts, 75
Zucchini-Pomodoro Topping, *168,* 169
tools, 55
for grilling pizza, 139
toppings, 160–179
Amatriciana, 165
Artichoke Pesto, 166
Caponata, 172
Cauliflower, Mashed, 173
creating your own pizza with, 179
Double Mushroom, 174, *175*
Moroccan, Instant, 171
Onion, Caramelized, 176
Plum Tomato, Roasted, 164
Ricotta and Spinach, Spiced, 163
Roasted Vegetable Sauce, 177
Rosemary-Garlic Pepperonata, 162
Shrimp and Black Bean, 170
tips for, 8
Tomato Compote, Winter, 178
White Bean, Spicy, 167
Zucchini-Pomodoro, *168,* 169
tortilla(s):
Green and White Tortillizzas, Simple, 146
Grilled Spanish, Pizza, 131
Hot and Spicy Mexican Tortillizzas, 145
Mini Mexi-Pizzas with Sole, 74
Pork Taco Pizzas, Spicy, *42,* 43
Seared-Salmon Pizzas with Arugula and Shaved

Parmesan, *68,* 69
Seven-Layer Taco Pizzas, 93
Southwestern Shrimp-and-Sausage Pizzas, 72, *73*
Tostada Pizzas with Beef and Black Beans, Tex-Mex, 53
tuna:
Focaccia Stuffed Pizza, 142, *143*
Niçoise on Potato-Rosemary Pizza, 58
Olive, and Roasted Pepper Pizza, 65
Tomato Pizza Melts, 75
turkey:
Alfredo-Saltimbocca Pizza with Asparagus, 40
Mexican Pizza Grande, 98
Pastrami Reuben Calzones, 116
pepperoni, in Pizza Rustica, 108, *109*
Smoked, Grilled Onion, and Tomato Pizza, 123
Twists, Pizza, with Tomato Dipping Sauce, *28,* 29

V

vegetable(s):
Curried, Pizza, 89
Grilled Summer, with Fresh Salsa, 195
Mixed, Pickles, 194
Roasted, and "Soysage" Deep-Dish Pizza, 83
Roasted, Sauce Topping, 177
Steamed Fall, with Garlic, 197
see also specific vegetables

W

white bean(s):
and Caponata Pizza, 147
and Sausage Pizza, Spicy, 130
Topping, Spicy, 167
Tuna, Olive, and Roasted Pepper Pizza, 65
White Clam Pizza, 66
Whole-Wheat Pizza Dough, 11

Y

yellow squash:
Grilled Summer Vegetables with Fresh Salsa, 195
Pizza Primavera, *100,* 101

Z

zucchini:
Grilled Summer Vegetables with Fresh Salsa, 195
Lemon-Thyme, on Flatbread, 135
Mediterranean Pan Pizza, 110
Pizza Primavera, *100,* 101
-Pomodoro Topping, *168,* 169